IN CAHOOTS, IN ASBURY PARK

Written By Josh Davidson

This book is dedicated to the brave men and women in uniform who have sacrificed their lives for our freedom, to the memory of Eugene and Rachel Davidson and Jean and Aaron Schwartz and to the Asbury Angels, including John Luraschi, John Oeser and George Theiss, who graciously contributed to this book.

Book Title & Contents Copyright © 2015 by Joshua Davidson. All Rights Reserved.

All rights reserved. No part of this book may be reproduced in any form or by any electronic or mechanical means including information storage and retrieval systems, without permission in writing from the author. The only exception is by a reviewer, who may quote short excerpts in a review.

Cover designed by Michelle Slevin, of PDI Designs
Front Cover photo by Michelle Slevin
Back Cover photo by Lewis Bloom

Written by Josh Davidson
Edited by Karl Vilacoba
Layout & design by Josh Davidson
with special thanks to Michael Burke, of Solari Creative, for design ideas and support
Photos by Lewis Bloom and Conni Freestone
Additional photo credits throughout the book

For information regarding concert dates and album purchases and other Boccigalupe & the Badboys history and facts, visit http://www.boccigalupemusic.com or https://www.facebook.com/Bocci123/
For more Lewis Bloom photos, go to http://www.lewisbloomphoto.com
For more Conni Freestone photos, go to http://www.connifreestone.com/conn
For more Michelle Paponetti Slevin graphics, go to http://www.pdidesignnj.com
View the work of Michael Burke and his team at http://www.solaricreative.com
View one of the best music history sites available at http://classicurbanharmony.net
Support local bands, live music and visit Asbury Park!

Paperback versions printed in the United States of America

First Printing: November 2018

CONTENTS

PREFACE 1
Chapter 1 *Up on the Roof* 12
Chapter 2 *Asbury Park, Growing Up* 19
Chapter 3 *Swing City* 35
Chapter 4 *"Booming" in Swing City* 42
Chapter 5 *A Drop of the Psychedelic* 54
Chapter 6 *High Times in Psychedelic City* 72
Chapter 7 *I Think I Can Get With This* 77
Chapter 8 *By the Strands of his Hair* 83
Chapter 9 *Schrebs* 91
Chapter 10 *The Audition* 96
Chapter 11 *Sidewalks* 106
Chapter 12 *In Cahoots* 114
Chapter 13 *A Storm Called Springsteen Strikes* 122
Chapter 14 *"Southside" Lays the Foundation* 129
Chapter 15 *In Cahoots, With New Jersey* 142
Chapter 16 *The Calculator* 155
Chapter 17 *Joy, Joan & the Asbury Fans* 162
Chapter 18 *The Souvenir* 169
Chapter 19 *"That Son of a Bitch"* 182
Chapter 20 *The Split* 191
Chapter 21 *The George Theiss Band* 198
Chapter 22 *The End of an Era* 203
Chapter 23 *Boccigalupe & the Badboys* 221
Chapter 24 *Bruce Stalkers* 234
Chapter 25 *After the Storm* 238
Chapter 26 *Where the Bands Are: The Clubs of Asbury Park* 251
Works Cited 263
Photo Credits 265
Acknowledgements 267
About the Author 269

PREFACE

"Oh my God! My momma told me about Asbury Park, what a beautiful place," June Carter Cash told Henry Vaccaro, Sr., as they discussed Vaccaro's experiences growing up in the City of Asbury Park, New Jersey.

Vaccaro, a lifelong Asbury resident and prominent developer, showed Carter Cash a picture of the Berkeley-Carteret Hotel, which he had planned to purchase and restore as they waited for the "Man in Black" to finish filming a movie in 1983. When Johnny returned to the bus, Vaccaro showed him pictures of other Asbury Park landmarks, including Convention Hall and the Paramount Theatre and explained his plans to restore the Berkeley-Carteret. The iconic artist was impressed.

"Henry, when you get that place, I want to open it up for you and it's not going to cost you a dime," Vaccaro recalled Johnny Cash saying.

"Johnny, I can't accept it," Vaccaro responded.
"What do you mean?" Cash said.

"I'm not your friend to take from you," Vaccaro said. "It will be my honor if you would open it up, but I want to pay you like everybody else pays you. If you want to take that money and make an investment in the hotel, then we've got a deal."

Josh Davidson

Shaking Vaccaro's hand Cash said, "Well, I'm going to have somebody check it out and if it works out, we have a deal." After showing Cash's accountant the area, hotel and financial documents associated with the deal, Cash became Vaccaro's first investor in the hotel during the next day. The Cashes fell immediately in love with the city and visited repeatedly throughout their lives. Vaccaro's brother, Sebastian, and another friend, television news anchor Ernie Anastos, eventually joined the $18 million restoration project. With the city in decline since the early 1970s, the investors paid only $330,000 for the hotel, which was closed for the previous six years. Only two other hotels, including the Monterey, were left standing, signifying the decay of the city that once attracted hundreds of thousands of visitors each summer. The city's other wood-based hotels were destroyed by either fire or lightning. The hotels and nearby residences once hosted the likes of Babe Ruth, Lou Gehrig, Frank Sinatra, Elizabeth Taylor and mobsters, including Frank Costello, Vito Genovese and Guarino "Willie" Moretti. During its heyday, no one left the city without dozens of lifelong memories that included swaying their hips to the jazz, rock or big band music blaring throughout its clubs or watching muscle cars speed across the circuit.

Vaccaro and his partners faced an uphill value, as they attempted to restore one of the city's vital landmarks to its old form. Some of the surviving hotels and facilities around them served as halfway houses for individuals diagnosed with mental illnesses.

"In the '70s and the early '80s, we had 1,600 mental patients living on the beachfront and walking the boardwalk and that really started the decline of everything," Vaccaro said. "People were afraid to come."

The amusements, food stands and rides that once attracted thousands of families to the city were closed. The small stores that once sold thousands of items along the boardwalk each summer were closed permanently and boarded up.

"That's why I bought the Berkley so cheap and I believe that was the cornerstone of the rebirth of the city," Vaccaro said.

The Berkeley-Carteret Hotel restoration project thrived from the onset and launched the Vaccaro brothers' effort to restore the remainder of the city.

"The Berkeley was an instant success," Henry Vaccaro said. "We restored the hotel to the grandeur of the 1920s. We restored the ballroom exactly as it was in 1926, with beautiful plaster moldings and antique chandeliers imported from Czechoslovakia."

Within the first year, they hired a general manager and food and beverage director from renowned establishments in New York City. During the initial four years, the hotel's food and beverage revenue exceeded that of any other business in New Jersey, but room occupancies were much fewer than desired, Vaccaro said. Many concertgoers visited the hotel to eat or drink after enjoying a national music act at the nearby Convention Hall. The visitors and even its owner reminisced about the city's glory days. In 1926, Vaccaro's grandfather, a landscape gardener, laid the hotel's grass. Vaccaro's parents were married at the hotel in 1939. He and his wife tied the knot at the Berkeley-Carteret 21 years later. In 1959, Pope Saint John XXIII traveled from Rome to oversee the testimonial of Vaccaro's father at the hotel.

In the mid-1980s, Vaccaro filed legal action to prevent the City Council from selling the entire beachfront, including Convention Hall, the boardwalk casino and every pavilion for $1 million. Vaccaro said he convinced the Council to add pre-qualifications into the bid in order to guarantee the project's success. An insurance salesman's bid was disqualified and Vaccaro won the contract to redevelop the city at a price of $500,000. However, the insurance salesman successfully protested the contract, as the assigned judge indicated the City could not require specific qualifications in the request for proposals for the stipulated type of property, Vaccaro said. Based on Vaccaro's recommendation, Asbury Park's mayor established a Redevelopment Authority. The authority redesigned the entire beachfront, before opening up the solicitation for bids.

In 1985, the Vaccaro brothers won the redevelopment contract with their new partner, Carabetta Enterprises, Inc., of Connecticut. The companies formed a partnership, known as Carabetta Vaccaro Developers LLC. Aside from the Berkeley-Carteret, the Vaccaro brothers purchased and restored 21 other properties, including the Palace Amusements Park, hotels, parking lots and business. The declining city experienced a brief period of hope, as visitors returned to reminisce and make new memories.

The rebirth lasted less than a handful of years. On 4th of July weekend in 1988, sewage and medical supplies washed ashore the beaches of Monmouth County, New Jersey, from Asbury Park to Avon. The waters were closed due to the discovery of high concentrations of bacteria. A month earlier, five blood vials emerged on the nearby beaches of Ortley Beach and Island Beach State Park, both in neighboring Ocean County. After formal tests were performed, officials announced that two of the vials had acquired immune deficiency syndrome (AIDS) antibodies. They announced that one tested positive for hepatitis. In Asbury Park, the beachgoer numbers rapidly dwindled, as did those of the nighttime crowds who were scared away by an increase in crimes, such as car break-ins. The city would experience yet another period of decline, as the beachfront turned into a virtual ghost town for the next five summer seasons.

The Berkley-Carteret hotel soon was among the many establishments impacted by the economic slide. When both of the banks that held the mortgage on the Berkeley-Carteret failed, the Vaccaro brothers offered the city government a debt restructure plan with a personal guarantee from all limited partners on the $6.5 million of remaining mortgage, Vaccaro said. The government declined and sold the hotel to another entity for $1 million. For the next three years, the once popular hotel served as a private educational institution, Vaccaro said.

Carabetta Enterprises purchased the Vaccaro brothers' shares of the redeveloped properties at a price of $1 million per year through nine years. Henry Vaccaro said he immediately thought money would never be an issue during the remainder of his life. However, by the early 1990s, the redevelopment project surrendered to the dwindling real estate market in Asbury Park. Carabetta Enterprises and subsequently Vaccaro filed for bankruptcy. In 2002, Vaccaro brokered a deal between his former partner, the city and Asbury Partners, so the latter could attempt to once again restore Asbury Park. A New York-based company, iStar Financial, has since purchased the redevelopment rights.

Vaccaro, who was born on 4th Avenue in Asbury Park in 1940, remains an outspoken advocate of restoring the city to its early prominence to this day. He founded his own construction company in Asbury Park at the age of 19. In 1962, he won a contract to dismantle the city's Sunset Pavilion, after it was mostly destroyed by a fire, as well as the bridge that connected the Pavilion to the Berkeley-Carteret Hotel. He subsequently won the contract to build the new Sunset Pavilion. He eventually performed $1 billion of construction jobs throughout New Jersey, including building Asbury Park's municipal complex and the Asbury Park Middle School.

Vaccaro made many memories in the city after his family moved to bordering Interlaken in 1946. By the early 1950s, he routinely walked the entire boardwalk, enjoying every single amusement park ride, before catching a show at the Mayfair or St. James theaters and returning home.

Josh Davidson

"If there was a job in Asbury, I wanted to do it, because it was my hometown," he said.

Vaccaro made his first investment in the music industry by purchasing Kramer Guitars, based in nearby Neptune, New Jersey, in 1976. In 1983, Kramer became the first company to endorse Van Halen. Eddie Van Halen used the guitars extensively and replaced the neck of his iconic black and white striped and red bodied "Frankenstrat" with a Kramer neck. In 1984, he scampered across the desks of a school library in the band's famous "Hot for Teacher" video soloing on his "Frankenstrat." Other notable Kramer artifacts include the aluminum axe-shaped bass developed for Gene Simmons of Kiss. Cash's bandmates began playing Kramer guitars onstage in 1977 after Cash and Vaccaro first met at the Garden State Arts Center, in Holmdel, New Jersey. The two men became close friends, spending many years touring the world together. Cash, a serious investor, returned frequently to Asbury Park, where he appeared at City Council meetings or spent time with his wife. Cash's family asked Vaccaro to serve as an honorary pall-bearer at Cash's funeral in 2003.

The story of the Asbury Park music scene converges at the railroad tracks of Springwood Avenue. From a social perspective, one might view two separate worlds, sometimes divided by race, on each side of the tracks. Usually excluded from the happenings in the east side resort areas which surrounded the boardwalk, many African-Americans who actually built the hotels and venues developed their own society on Asbury's west side beginning in the early 1900s. Many African-Americans felt they were not afforded the same opportunities as whites on the east side. Though some African-American musicians experienced similar treatment by east side club owners, race was a non-issue among musicians of any background, said Tony Amato, former keyboardist/vocalist of the now disbanded musical group Cahoots. Vacccaro is Amato's godfather.

IN CAHOOTS, IN ASBURY PARK

Amato currently performs with his current band Boccigalupe & the Badboys.

Since an early age, Amato observed racial tension, which centered around the exclusion of African-Americans from many of the activities that occurred on the east side of the city. He noticed invisible boundary lines, such as the northeast side of the city, where he only saw African-Americans of his age walking to and returning from school. Many of their parents were only permitted to work in the hotels and establishments of the east side. The recreational amenities, as well as the more lucrative jobs, quality of life and housing of the east side were off limits to many African-Americans, Amato said.

"I don't think Joe Mattice, the mayor at the time, understood or tried to help the people," he said.

This wrongful treatment gradually fueled a buildup of racial tension throughout the years, Amato said. The tension forced Amato and his white friends to carefully choose their walking paths. Yet the power and collaboration of music broke through many of the racial barriers. Music was a common interest among many of the city's youth, who didn't care about the color of one's skin during jam sessions or gigs. Still, few African-Americans ventured to the east side to play, though some members of the white community crossed the tracks on occasion. Though many received the evil eye, their African-American counterparts ensured they were protected when danger arose.

"They would stand up for you," Amato said.

The white musicians strived to transcend any barriers. They wanted no part of the old ways of thinking that encouraged the racism around them.

"Our group of musicians in the community at the time didn't get involved in such bullshit," Amato said.

Regardless of race, musicians shared a common interest — forgetting the tension that surrounded them.

"There was a musicians' mindset versus a citizen's mindset," Amato said. "They didn't have a connection like the musicians experienced. The music was the main thing that connected the east and west side of Asbury and it still does."

At the age of 18, Amato met Norman Perkins, an African-American bassist from Washington Avenue on the west side. The two musicians shared a common interest in fusion music and formed a band. The facial expressions of people in clubs outside of the Asbury Park area were indicative of the lack of acceptance of the African-American bassist. However, Amato and his bandmates focused solely on the immense talent evident in Perkins' musical chops. The musicians of the east side never hesitated to ask Perkins to cross the railroad tracks and jam.

Though musicians didn't consider race when auditioning potential band members, some African-American musicians didn't receive the performance opportunities afforded to white musicians by east side club owners, Amato said.

By the early 1960s through the 1970s, racial tension reached a boiling point throughout the country. In August 1965, a six-day race riot spurred by claims of unfair treatment and police brutality destroyed the Watts neighborhood of Los Angeles, resulting in 34 deaths, more than 1,000 injuries and $40 million in property damage. In July of 1967, six days of riots sparked by claims of racial profiling by police, exclusion of minorities from political entities and a lack of job opportunities led to 26 deaths and hundreds of injuries in Newark, New Jersey. Nearly three years later, rioters from Newark, traveled south to stir the pot and initiate the riots in Asbury Park, according to Tom Gilmour, Asbury Park's former director of economic development.

IN CAHOOTS, IN ASBURY PARK

During the nearly weeklong chaos involving thousands of rioters, at least 165 people were injured and more than 130 were arrested, according to a July 9, 1970 report by *The Daily Register* newspaper of Monmouth County. Property damage estimates exceeded $2 million, the paper reported. The Salvation Army distributed sandwiches and coffee to local residents and the Welfare Board brought food to local churches. Police fired warning shots above the heads of crowding rioters and wounded 92 people with shotgun pellets.

During the riots, the New Jersey State Police and Army National Guard circled around the west side, preventing much of the damage from occurring on the opposite side of the Springwood Avenue railroad tracks. Struggling to contain the situation, the state ordered the closure of all businesses on the east side, Amato said.

As the riots became imminent, jamming together or even mingling was not as easy for African-American and white musicians. The white musicians were pressured against bringing African-American musicians to the east side and vice versa. The forced segregation prevented musicians of separate backgrounds and influences from sharing their talents. At one point, Amato's four-person band that was evenly split with white and African-American musicians could not rehearse for two weeks due to the racial tension surrounding them. The tension, which didn't break for nearly three years, prevented the blending of talented of musicians of separate races.

Josh Davidson

Some members of Cahoots in the late 1970s. (from left to right) Steve Schraeger (drums), John Luraschi (bass), George Theiss (vocals/rhythm guitar), Tony Amato (keyboards/vocals) and John Oeser (singer/percussionist). (Photo courtesy of Lisa Ferrara)

In Cahoots, In Asbury Park, tells the story of one band, Cahoots, and its drive to beat the odds of the music industry in a city that has endured great triumph and despair since its founding in 1871. The book follows the lives and careers of Amato, bassist John Luraschi, singer/percussionist John Oeser, rhythm guitarist/vocalist George Theiss, keyboardist Michael Scialfa, drummer Steve Schraeger and saxophonist Tommy LaBella, telling the city's story through their eyes, as they encounter other critical members of the city's music scene, including the musicians, fans and club owners.

The book begins with a story of Luraschi and his counterparts protecting the Upstage on Cookman Avenue during the riots. The book delves further into other important pieces of Asbury history, including the clubs and attractions on both sides of the tracks, before introducing each additional member of Cahoots. Readers will learn about the significance the city had on Cahoots' career, as well as the careers of other legendary artists, including Bruce Springsteen, Bon Jovi, "Little" Steven Van Zandt and Southside Johnny & The Asbury Jukes. For its

IN CAHOOTS, IN ASBURY PARK

rich music history, Asbury Park stands as one of the most vibrant and eclectic music scenes in the world. Similar to Liverpool, where the Beatles launched their career in the United Kingdom, and Seattle, where bands like Pearl Jam, Nirvana and Soundgarden made their names, Asbury Park has its own unique identity, which no city will ever replicate. Local and national bands continue to fill clubs, such as The Saint, Wonder Bar and the legendary Stone Pony. Today, on both sides of the Springwood Avenue tracks, fans can enjoy music with no racial boundaries or pressure to stand on one side of the city.

Chapter 1
Up on the Roof

"It was devastating...People were destroying their own property." - Ernest "Boom" Carter, musician

On a hot summer night in July 1970, the alliance of musicians who formed a bond in Asbury Park stood together to support their headquarters. The riots, which began on July 4, were already destroying parts of the city surrounding Springwood Avenue. Sensing the mayhem would progress about a half-dozen blocks south and spill onto the Cookman Avenue section, a young bassist named John Luraschi and a slew of other musicians took tactical positions on the stairwells and roof of The Upstage.

As some guarded the roof of their rock n' roll castle with shotguns wedged between their young arms, they were prepared to engage anyone who dared to penetrate the landmark that was so important to them. Their mission was to prevent the rioters from hurling firebombs into the club, which stood at 700 Cookman Ave., intersected by Bond Street.

Luraschi seized the opportunity to join the squad of rock n' roll soldiers who stood guard and to return a favor to the venue's owners, a pair of married hairdressers named Tom and Margaret Potter, who had never hesitated to support him and his colleagues.

"They always gave me a few dollars for playing, so I could eat and do whatever I needed to do," Luraschi said. "They always looked out for me."

Nothing ever came easy for Luraschi. He had lost both of his parents in his early 20s and survived on the support and mentorship of the many "guardian angels" who had entered his life. The Potters were among the many Asbury Park proprietors who provided Luraschi with endless guidance and assistance and asked for little-to-nothing in return.

After days of camping out at Tom Potter's nearby home, Luraschi now stared at the city's streets from the roof of The Upstage, hoping the presence of him and the alliance would sway the incoming rioters to pass by without harming the venue. He noticed his prized possession, a 1948 Harley Davidson Knucklehead motorcycle, was parked next to the sidewalk in front of the club.

Luraschi felt helpless as he heard the footsteps and voices of the rioters. If he left his position to protect or move his bike, he would expose himself and his friends to the violence being inflicted upon the city.

"Oh no, my bike!" yelled Luraschi, who had previously spent countless hours restoring the motorcycle. The angels that surrounded Luraschi that day, both among the living and potentially the deceased, held their ground.

"Everybody came flying around the street and nobody even touched the bike," Luraschi recalled. "They all went around it."

The rioters continued past The Upstage, broke some glass and inflicted minor structural damage to a nearby storefront, before they continued down Cookman Avenue. Luraschi's motorcycle and The Upstage were left untouched.

"It survived," said Luraschi of the bike. "It was amazing. It was like there was light around it."

Bands were established and musicians began their musical journeys at The Upstage. Nobody knew that some of them, like Bruce Springsteen, Steven Van Zandt and "Southside" Johnny Lyon would become celebrities one day.

"I met a lot of great players here," Luraschi said. "There were a lot of alliances made here."

From the west side of Asbury Park, divided by the railroad tracks along Springwood Avenue, drummer Ernest "Boom" Carter experienced the riots from a different perspective. Whereas Luraschi and his friends saw their musical stomping ground spared from the mayhem that was overtaking the city, Carter wasn't as lucky as he sat in front of Asbury Park High School on Sunset Avenue. There, he witnessed the complete demolition of the music clubs on the west side where he had first met those jazz legends who became his mentors, like drummer Joe Dukes. Around him, many other hard working men and women of Springwood Avenue also watched as their hopes and dreams vanished.

It was about 30 years prior when Asbury Park's African-Americans built their own community, centered on Springwood Avenue, in response to the racial segregation that plagued the country. Only allowed to work inside the jazz clubs, hotels and other venues on the east side, they constructed jazz clubs like the Orchid Lounge, owned by Odyssey Moore, on the east end of Springwood Avenue and Leo Karp's Turf

IN CAHOOTS, IN ASBURY PARK

Club on the corner of Springwood and Atkins avenues. Big Bill's and The Madonna Club were other major west side venues where young, budding musicians realized their dreams in the presence of legends. Within the bustling community, African-American men and women, who worked countless hours to provide for their families, wore long dresses and heels and fancy suits, ties and hats as they listened to some of the planet's greatest jazz musicians perform. The fruits of their labor allowed them to afford expensive outfits and vehicles, made by Chevrolet, Pontiac and Cadillac. But the riots brought a sense of despair and uncertainty to the many African-Americans who sacrificed their time and life savings to open businesses in the west side.

As his father Joseph A. Carter, Sr., an *Asbury Park Press* photographer, used his camera to document the destruction of the many local businesses his friends had sacrificed so much to build, "Boom" and his friends made one final attempt to keep the music alive. As the rioting continued, Carter and his band of hippies sat in front of Asbury Park High School playing guitars and bongos. Surrounded by some visual artists who sat and painted, the musicians of a variety of races ignored the chaos, racism and violence around them and jammed.

"Everybody else was going crazy, but we were out there on the campus, just making music," Carter said. "We were just playing."

"We don't need this," they told one another as the nationwide racial tension swept through Asbury.

"I think we were a little bit ahead of our time on that thought, because we had so much fun before all of this," said Carter, of his friends' decision to stay away from the violence.

During the preceding years, Carter and his friends had spent hours together, discovering one another through music.

"When all of this crap was going down, nobody knew what to do or how to act," he said. "You didn't know who your friend was and who wasn't. It just blew everything up."

In the summer of 1970, Carter's life resembled a seven-inch record, emanating beautiful music as it slowly spins and scrapes against the sharp needle above. But on July 4, the music and life Carter had known previously came to a screeching halt. The metaphoric record spun in all the wrong directions before shattering to pieces on the streets of Asbury Park's west side.

"It was devastating," said Carter, who had just completed his senior year at Asbury Park High School. "There were fires. People were destroying their own property. It was just total ignorance."

A short time before, a diverse mixture of Greeks, Jews, Italians and Chinese people lived together in unity in Asbury Park's neighborhoods.

"When the riots came down, everybody started separating and going on their own, so to speak," he said.

Carter was shocked by the segregation that now overtook the once diverse section of the city. In the aftermath, many white residents left Asbury Park.

"My father had eight millimeter film of the riots," Carter said. "He was so ashamed of what was going down, he didn't let anybody ever see it. He even told my sister not to show anybody else or to even destroy it, because he was so ashamed."

Carter's sister, Madonna Carter Jackson, has released two editions of the book *Asbury Park: A West Side Story: A Pictorial Journey Through the Eyes of Joseph A. Carter, Sr.*, which through her deceased father's photographs vividly depicts the story of early prosperity and later despair on Springwood Avenue. Joseph Carter invited community members of any race into his studio, where he captured the memories of their lives.

IN CAHOOTS, IN ASBURY PARK

"He was such a down to earth guy," Boom recalled. "He had no hate or discord for anybody. He was just a beautiful man. He helped anybody that he could."

Along with his mother, who worked as a seamstress in Asbury Park for more than 20 years, Carter's parents worked tirelessly to house, feed, clothe and provide for their family.

His father's photography studio on Springwood Avenue only had minor damage from the riots. Knowing the business was owned by a respected member of the community, most of the rioters left it alone.

"A lot of black businesses were destroyed unintentionally and then some maybe intentionally, I don't know," Carter said. "It was just totally stupid to destroy your own home because you're pissed off."

The historic clubs where Carter learned the art of swing music were destroyed beyond repair. Some were burned to the ground. Springwood Avenue would never return to its original form and the music scene on the west side suddenly vanished. Even today, Carter remains devastated by the demise of a city block that meant so much to him.

"When it went away, I realized how important it was," he said. "After the riots – it just changed the world for us."

From the roof of an Asbury Park surfboard shop, Springsteen and local drummer Vini "Mad Dog" Lopez, who would later join him as the original drummer in the E Street Band, helplessly watched the destruction within the 1.6-square-mile city. Before The Upstage opened, Springsteen spent a lot of time in Asbury Park becoming acclimated to the music scene. He was heavily influenced by the jazz players on the west side. "Little" Steven Van Zandt joined Springsteen on many trips across the railroad tracks.

"They would listen to and study music there and then bring it back to The Upstage and share it with the other musicians they jammed with at night," said Eileen Chapman, Monmouth University's associate director of Performing Arts and former manager of The Stone Pony, Mrs. Jay's and The Fast Lane in Asbury Park. "So, there came to be that specific sound to try to kind of incorporate the old jazz and blues of the west side into what the younger musicians were doing here at that time."

East side musicians, such as Springsteen and "Southside" Johnny Lyon, had a pre-established affection for soul and blues music before they began venturing over to the west side, said Robert Santelli, an author and journalist who has covered Asbury Park extensively since the 1970s. British Invasion bands like the Rolling Stones and The Animals gave many young musicians and fans an understanding of the genre, he said.

As racial tension intensified in the years that preceded the riots, only a few east side musicians had the courage to cross the train tracks into the west side. Those who did only made the trips on rare occasions, said Santelli, who is currently the executive director of the Grammy Museum at L.A. Live, in Los Angeles.

Santelli had many African-American friends when he attended the very integrated Memorial High School, in West New York, New Jersey. The school exposed him to the racial tension that was spreading across urban America, before he moved to Point Pleasant Beach. There were only two African-American students in the entire Jersey Shore town's high school.

Santelli's father, a state trooper who was on duty for the riots in the New Jersey cities of Newark, Camden and Jersey City, banned his son from going to the west side. Santelli only made rare day trips to the west side's record stores.

"It was too dangerous," Santelli said. "The vibe wasn't right. If you were a hippie and a musician, you kind of got a little leeway, but not people like me or my friends. That wasn't something that we would normally do."

Chapter 2
Asbury Park, Growing Up

"In our minds they were as good, if not better, than Led Zeppelin, which was the ultimate compliment." - Robert Santelli, Executive Director, Grammy Museum, regarding the local band Steel Mill

As a pre-teen in the mid-1960s, Luraschi spent many joyful moments with his family in Asbury Park. The city was filled with crowded fresh and saltwater pools, music clubs, sugary junk food, restaurants, arcades filled with games and pinball machines and other carnival-style rides and attractions that made living fun.

"When I was kid, my parents used to go to Florida and I used to get mad, because there was nothing else that I wanted do when I was 10 or

12 except come down to Asbury with my friends," Luraschi said. "This was the best thing there was. There was always something to do."

The city already had a history of growth and renaissance since 1871, when it was founded by a New York City broom manufacturer named James A. Bradley. With ties to the neighboring municipality of Ocean Grove, the developer had a vision for creating a prodigious resort town on the Jersey Shore, Gilmour said. As he developed what became known as Asbury Park, Bradley brought with him some of the neighboring municipality's puritanical views, but set aside some of those viewpoints, such as those which would have restricted the sale of alcohol, Gilmour said. Adult beverages were critical to the economic success of local hotels.

It wasn't long before vacationers from throughout the country were staying in Asbury Park's more than 100 hotels, as the city was transformed into a premier East Coast destination. The city was in a convenient location for people who wanted to stop at the beach on their way to New York, Gilmour said. Since railroad tracks ran across the Jersey Shore, Asbury Park and Long Branch became hot spots for people who wanted to stop at the beach on their way to points throughout the Northeast. People who traveled to Philadelphia went further south to the New Jersey beaches in Wildwood and Atlantic City.

In the early 1900s, more than 100,000 people visited the city during the summer. Two separate train stations provided transportation to residents and vacationers. Big bands provided the musical backdrop for young couples who packed the dance floors inside hotel bars on Asbury Park's east side. The internationally renowned big band leader, trombonist and soloist with the John Phillip Sousa Band, from Saint Joseph, Missouri, Arthur Pryor, settled in Asbury Park when he wasn't performing throughout the world. Sousa composed and conducted patriotic marches during the late Romantic era. In an effort to rival the free concerts by famous brass musicians on the pavilions and bandstands of Coney Island, New York, the city hired Pryor to perform at its band shell.

During the 1940s and 1950s, bands on the east side of the city played the popular music of the United States, Gilmour said. This included big band music in the late 1930s and early 1940s, until doo wop took its influence from jazz and joined rock n' roll as Asbury Park's popular music style in the mid-1950s through the 1960s.

In Asbury Park, the portion of Cookman Avenue that ran between Ocean Avenue and Kingsley Street and extended across the city was known as "The Circuit." In this area at various times in the 1900s, bars such as Mrs. Jay's, The Wonder Bar, Gold Digger, Steve Brody's, Jerry's Tavern, The Student Prince, Rainbow Room and Finaldi's, opened their doors to rock n' roll music fans on almost every other block. Some stayed open for years, while others had a short lifespan. Despite the close vicinity of clubs, patrons of the 1950s would normally stay in the same venue rather than bar hop from one to the next, said Carol Wuestoff, who was born and raised in and rarely left the city.

Wuestoff met many out-of-towners, also known as "Bennies" to the locals, when she hung out at Terry's Bar and Tavern, owned by her family on Kingsley Street. There, Wuestoff's sister waited on Judy Garland, one of many celebrities and athletes who vacationed in Asbury Park during the summer. The tavern was located one block away from Mrs. Jay's, which opened in 1932 in the building where the legendary Stone Pony rock club stands today, at 913 Ocean Ave. During the 1950s, Mrs. Jay's shared the building with a sub shop next door and a liquor store on the corner, Wuestoff said. Mrs. Jay's eventually occupied the whole building. From the 1930s-1940s, Mrs. Jay's hosted the same style of big band music played at Asbury Park's boardwalk casino and Convention Hall during the era. Rumored visits by Frank Sinatra and other music industry legends remain a part of the club's folklore. Today, the club is a conversation topic in jazz circles throughout the world.

The upper deck of the Fun House in Asbury's Palace Amusements in the late 1970s. (Photo by Lewis Bloom)

From the 1950s through the early 1960s, Asbury Avenue was jammed with cars during the weekend, Wuestoff said. Asbury Avenue was the city's major throughway, which most visitors accessed via Route 35 in Neptune. Upon arrival, they left their cars in a parking spot until they exited the city, since most of the tiny city was accessible via foot. The crowds let up in the winter when many of the activities dwindled.

The 36,000-square-foot Palace Amusements complex stood at the southern end of the boardwalk. The facility housed a merry-go-round, Ferris wheel and ice skating rink, along with other rides, frightening fun houses, arcade games and festivities. Gambling with real money was prohibited in the nearby boardwalk casino. Wuestoff and her friends swam at the natatorium building, which housed a swimming pool, on 3rd

IN CAHOOTS, IN ASBURY PARK

Avenue and in the outdoor saltwater Monte Carlo Pool, near 8th Avenue, where a tunnel led patrons directly to the beach. With other pools and attractions scoured across the city, Wuestoff and her friends had no need to leave the city for entertainment.

"In the summer time, the boardwalk and beaches were always packed," Wuestoff said.

"It was just the 'in' place to be at that time."

On Wednesdays, Wuestoff met her friends at Liggett's Drug Store and soda shop, on Cookman Avenue, before venturing downtown for the remainder of the night. They spent Friday nights at the movies, while the rest of their time was occupied either at the boardwalk or on the beach.

In the 1950s, family movies were shown in the city's many movie theaters, some of which included balconies and multi-level seating. They included The Mayfair, St. James, Lyric and Baronet Theatres.

"The movie theaters were beautiful," Wuestoff said. "They were very elaborate in those days."

The Paramount Theatre, which still hosts movies and music today, was built in a large convention complex, which included Convention Hall. Known for having deceptive skills on the hardwood, the basketball showboating troupe The Harlem Globetrotters were a major attraction during its bi-annual performances at The Paramount, Wuestoff said. Rather than the musical concerts that fill Convention Hall today, the venue hosted convention style events, such as boat shows, until the mid-1950s, Wuestoff said.

In July of 1956, rock music in Asbury Park almost met its demise when Convention Hall hosted its first African-American rock n' roll act, Frankie Lymon & The Teenagers. Teenagers from all races and various locations packed Convention Hall to catch the five-piece act. They caught a glimpse of one of the first teenaged rock n' roll acts, which scored six top 10 singles within 18 months, according to the *Billboard* charts, and was best known for its first hit single, "Why Do Fools Fall in Love."

"The venue's security was not what it could have been," said Dr. Charles Horner, a music historian with Classic Urban Harmony, LLC. "They didn't have enough security and some fights broke out."

After only a few songs, the city's police stopped the concert and sent the entire young audience to the boardwalk.

"Of course, there were a lot of disgruntled teenagers who had come from long distances in order to see The Teenagers and now all of the sudden they were all pushed out on the boardwalk, at the same time," Horner said. "So there were fights, there was a minor riot and some people were arrested. It was not as big as it was made out to be. It was more of a disturbance than a riot, but it certainly shook everybody up."

The Asbury Park City Council seriously considered banning rock n' roll from the city.

"It never happened, but it came close to that," Horner said.

The council should have first determined the artist's musical style before deciding on which genre to ban. If they had, a ban on doo wop may have reached a vote. Many music fans have debated whether the group should be classified as rock n' roll or doo wop. During an interview for this book, Tony Amato, Cahoots' keyboardist, even texted singer Bobby Rydell to help classify the group.

"I think Frankie Lymon was more rock than doo wop. Just look at his record career. Don't know if I'm right, but who gives a fuck," Rydell responded.

Wuestoff grew up in a time when crime was non-existent and pride in one's community was predominant in the city. Families mobbed Asbury Park every year for its Easter Parade. Numerous artists, including Rydell, entertained the city's visitors and residents at its many venues.

IN CAHOOTS, IN ASBURY PARK

"It was nice growing up in Asbury, because for us there was always something going on," Wuestoff said. "I was related to three quarters of the town, so I always had some place to go to."

Wuestoff, who lived on 3rd and Central avenues, could walk with her friends across the boardwalk or downtown, during the day or evening, without any worries of becoming a crime victim. Fights or other disturbances were a rarity inside the bars during the era, she said.

"I don't think we ever locked our doors," Wuestoff said. "It's the way it was. You lived in the same neighborhood for most of your life. Everybody knew each other and nobody was afraid of anything."

Gates prevented cars from accessing the neighboring city of Ocean Grove during the weekends, Wuestoff said. Once the clock struck midnight on Saturday, visitors could only enter Ocean Grove via foot until Sunday passed.

Since the numerous shopping malls that exist throughout New Jersey today were nonexistent, Asbury Park's shopping district, which was centered around Steinbach's department store on Cookman Avenue, always drew large crowds of shoppers.

Wuestoff attended Asbury Park's Bradley Elementary School and Asbury Park High School, before moving to the nearby Ocean Township in 1968. Until then, she had not noticed any signs of the decay that plagued Asbury Park just years later. The retiree from the U.S. Army's former Fort Monmouth installation, located about 10 miles north of Asbury Park, currently lives in South Carolina.

Popular music heard throughout the city in the 1940s and 1950s closely paralleled that which dominated the remainder of the country, where jazz was evolving into to bebop or fast-paced jazz that focused on improvisation. Some small blues combos were heard throughout the city. Rhythm and blues music, which started to sweep the nation in the early 1950s, dominated the entire city throughout the decade. Rock n' roll music dominated the city's live music scene in the mid-1960s. With so many clubs providing opportunities to bands by then, musicians ventured to Asbury from throughout New Jersey looking to take advantage of the likely odds of landing a gig. Asbury Park was the optimal location for musicians looking to join a pre-established band or those who hoped to find solid musicians and build a band.

"The reason that Asbury Park really took off was there were just so many musicians down here and so many places to play that if you were a musician and you were trying to make it you wanted to be here," Gilmour said.

However, showing up at a club unannounced and expecting to play was not likely in the mid-1960s. Bands mostly had to book their gigs in advance.

"More than likely you could finagle your way in to play an afternoon show or something like that and hopefully you would invite your friends to come, so that it looked like the place was packed and then the owner would hire you at night," Gilmour said.

Band promotion became more formalized when Steel Mill gained local notoriety, said Tom Matthews, a longtime and loyal fan of the Asbury Music scene. In Asbury Park, local fans grew accustomed to top quality music in a culturally transforming region. Steel Mill was one of Bruce Springsteen's early bands.

"There was something in the air," Matthews said. "It was kind of like a mini renaissance."

In the 1960s, without a major venue in New Jersey to see bands like the PNC Bank Arts Center in Holmdel, of today, Convention Hall became the standard place to see national acts outside of Atlantic City, and drew bands like The Rolling Stones and The Who, Matthews said. The world's largest acts played 3,500 seat venues, such as Convention Hall, and didn't need to worry about filling a 20,000 seat arena, Matthews

IN CAHOOTS, IN ASBURY PARK

said. In August 1969, Led Zeppelin turned down a slot at the Woodstock Festival at Max Yasgur's farm in Bethel, New York, and instead headlined the "Summer of Stars" concert series at Convention Hall. Sound quality at Convention Hall depended upon the type of band on stage, Matthews said. For example, concertgoers got an exceptional auditory experience at an Emerson, Lake and Palmer show. The Hall was uniquely built as a sound chamber for the pipe organ, so the band successfully manipulated the venue's acoustics and performed solidly, Matthews said.

Sonny Kenn was one of the first artists to have an immense impact on Asbury Park's music scene of the 1960s. Kenn and his family moved three miles south to Belmar in 1962. After giving up the trumpet to play the electric guitar in the eighth grade, Kenn, Richie Tomes and Chuck Anderson formed his first band, called The Electrons. The band became Sonny and the Sounds, before adding Vini Lopez on the drums and becoming Sonny and the Starfires. In 1966, the band played the Hullabaloo club in a former hotel garage on Kingsley Street. Hullabaloos were large warehouses that were converted into dance clubs and existed in most counties throughout the state. The group was hired to play other Hullabaloo clubs along the East Coast, covering songs by artists such as The Beatles, Animals, Wilson Pickett and The Rolling Stones.

In 1967, guitarist/vocalist Bill Chinnock, and keyboard player/future E Street Band member Danny Federici also hit the Hullabaloo circuit with The Storytellers in Monmouth County and became a popular band on the Jersey Shore. Their next project, the Downtown Tangiers Rocking Rhythm & Blues Band, also included Lopez and bassist Wendell John. Another future E Streeter, Garry Tallent, eventually replaced John, before Down Tangiers disbanded. Keeping Tallent on bass, Chinnock added David Sancious on keyboards and "Big" Bobby Williams on drums to form Glory Road.

Josh Davidson

Springsteen was a geographically challenged guitar slinger before he shook up the Asbury scene in the late 1960s. Springsteen's trip from his hometown of Freehold Borough to Asbury Park was a lengthy one, Santelli said. Many other of Freehold's young adults trekked from their hometown to Asbury Park, where they surfed and strolled the boardwalk, but lived too far inland to become an organic part of the popular beach and surf communities, Santelli said. Springsteen didn't own a car and couldn't make enough repeated 15-mile trips back and forth to the city to become a recognized name, unlike Lopez, who was already well-known on the Asbury boardwalk. Following the disbandment of the Freehold-based Castiles, Springsteen formed Earth in 1968, which included bassist John Graham and drummer Michael Burke, who Springsteen had met while attending Ocean County College in Toms River, New Jersey.

During that summer, Springsteen began jamming at The Upstage. Spotting the fast-playing guitar phenomenon leading a jam at the club, Lopez and Federici worked on convincing Springsteen to leave Earth to form a new band with them. Time had passed and, in 1969, Springsteen formed Child, a blues-based, rock band which included Federici on organ, Lopez on drums and Vinnie Roslin on bass. Managed by a local Challenger East Surfboards company owner from the San Francisco Bay Area, Carl "Tinker" West, the rock band soon changed its name to Steel Mill.

Steel Mill consistently impressed its strong contingent of fans. Santelli recalled attending the Led Zeppelin show at Convention Hall in 1969, where many future E Street Band members also sat in the audience. All of the Asbury Park musicians in attendance were "absolutely blown away" by the British rock band, he said. Shortly after, Santelli watched Steel Mill perform at Ocean County College. The once again amazed student told his friend: "You know I love Led Zeppelin, but Steel Mill's better."

IN CAHOOTS, IN ASBURY PARK

"It just blew us away that this was a local band that no one knew about," Santelli said. "In our minds they were as good, if not better, than Led Zeppelin, which was the ultimate compliment."

During a performance at The Sunshine Inn in Asbury Park, the headlining band, Cactus, walked on stage and stood before a crowd that was left astonished by the opening act, Steel Mill, recalled Rich Kelly, an early Asbury Park music fan.

"They were so good; it was unbelievable," said Kelly of the opener. "Nobody wanted Cactus to come on. So when Cactus finally came on stage they said, 'My God, those guys were great. Thanks for letting us play.'"

Cactus was a nationally known act, which featured members of the rock group Vanilla Fudge.

West played an integral role in Steel Mill's success. He offered a sense of business acumen that Asbury Park's musicians lacked, Santelli said. West immediately recognized Springsteen's immense talent and offered to manage him, he said. West was the only real band manager on the Jersey Shore, whereas other managers were band acquaintances who primarily carried equipment to gigs. Springsteen's new manager offered knowledge, expertise and money. He also offered a place to stay and perform at his surf shop.

"He was an extremely smart person," Santelli said. "Just his intellect and his IQ is still to this day something to be admired. Tinker was the only notable person, at least from my point of view, that had any business sense at all and thankfully he put that business sense to use with Bruce, back then."

Steel Mill traveled to California where it played local and major venues, such as The Fillmore in San Francisco. In California, the band was offered a less than modest recording contract by promoter Bill

Graham. West had many connections and was able to get Steel Mill the deal.

"They turned it down, rightfully so," Santelli said. "It wasn't a good deal at all."

The band returned to the East Coast and started to fall apart. Roslin left the band and was replaced on bass by Steven Van Zandt, who was raised in Middletown Township, New Jersey.

Springsteen disbanded Steel Mill in 1971 and with Van Zandt on guitar, formed a soul-rock band, called the Bruce Springsteen Band, by the following year. The band also included a horn section, female backup singers, Lopez on drums, Sancious on keyboards, Federici on organ and Tallent on bass.

"Boom" Carter witnessed his first Springsteen performance with the aforementioned band at Brookdale Community College in Lincroft, New Jersey. Armed with a Fender Telecaster in a band that bared a sonic resemblance to Derek and the Dominos, "The Boss" demonstrated the charisma for which he is known today, Carter said.

"He was throwing that out there then," Carter said. "He had a nice crowd listening to him."

Springsteen almost simultaneously formed the quirky, experimental alter ego project, Dr. Zoom and the Sonic Boom. Springsteen's five Bruce Springsteen Band bandmates joined him in Dr. Zoom, which was a gargantuan-sized act that also included Lyon on harmonica, "Big" Danny Gallagher on a variety of instruments, Williams on a second set of drums and many other musicians, including Luraschi, said Albany Al "Albee" Tellone, who played tenor saxophone with the band. The same five Bruce Springsteen Band bandmates and sometimes Springsteen joined Joe Hagstrom and Lyon in the Sundance Blues Band. Springsteen played lead guitar and sang when his schedule permitted and Van Zandt navigated the fret board of the bottleneck guitar.

IN CAHOOTS, IN ASBURY PARK

Though he was big and stocky, Gallagher was a very gentle man, Matthews recalled.

"He had a real presence when he was on stage," Matthews said. "He definitely got your attention."

Dr. Zoom was formed after the owner of Asbury's Sunshine Inn called West and offered Steel Mill a slot opening for the Allman Brothers, Tellone said. West told the owner that Steel Mill had disbanded and the Bruce Springsteen Band wasn't ready to perform in public. After the owner told West he wanted Springsteen at the venue, regardless of his supporting cast, Van Zandt and Springsteen decided to bring all of their friends from The Upstage together to form a festive, performance art style band, where the members wore costumes and girls twirled batons. Piggybacking off the Allman Brothers' dual drummer concept, the band included two drummers, lead guitarists, keyboardists and saxophone players. Inspired by regular games of Monopoly at Tellone's apartment, the band jokingly added a live Monopoly match to its stage show, Tellone said.

"There was talk of having Eddie Luraschi work on a motorcycle onstage too, but we nixed that quickly," Tellone said.

Eddie was John Luraschi's brother and a former bouncer at The Upstage.

The band played former Steel Mill songs, such as "Going Back to Georgia" and "Lady from Boston," and a new original entitled "Jambalaya."

"With the short rehearsal time available, we played some standard jam tunes too," Tellone said. "The lyrics of the originals were all Bruce's and none of us knew how he was capable of writing so many, just like he still does."

For Matthews, Dr. Zoom's performances stood out as something special. The band's psychedelic style resembled Iron Butterfly, infused with a rhythm and blues flavor, he said.

"They were pretty amazing," he said. "It was just big, impressive and tight for being that size. It didn't just sound like a bunch of guys they dragged together and threw up on the stage, which is essentially what it was. They had all been playing together in little groups. All of those pieces had been together at one point or another. I guess that's why it worked."

The aftermath of the riots had taken its toll on Asbury Park in the early 1970s, Santelli said. As all of the west side clubs were destroyed, many clubs on the east side had closed. Nothing was the same. The Upstage closed forever on Oct. 30, 1971, and many of its former patrons were becoming older, starting families and preparing for the next phases of their lives. The Asbury music scene began to suffer significantly, he said.

"The whole economic energy of Asbury Park had been eliminated with the riots," Santelli said.

Since they performed original music and were more sizable than normal, The Bruce Springsteen Band struggled to get gigs, he said.

"No one would hire them," Santelli said. "They were hardly making any money at all and it was clear that they just couldn't go on."

Many of Springsteen's friends and musical colleagues from Asbury, including Lyon, Lopez, Carter, Sancious, Tallent and Van Zandt, headed to Richmond, Virginia, to perform in a city where Steel Mill and other Jersey shore bands had been already warmly welcomed, Santelli said.

"And Bruce does something totally radical," Santelli said. "He does his thing without a band and starts commuting up to New York City and playing clubs up there like the Bitter End."

IN CAHOOTS, IN ASBURY PARK

After disbanding the Bruce Springsteen Band and Dr. Zoom in 1972, Springsteen traveled back forth from New Jersey to New York City's Greenwich Village via bus and performed with his acoustic guitar in the singer/songwriter scene. Though always adamant about his Jersey roots, Springsteen played at clubs like Kenny's Castaways, at 157 Bleeker St., which closed in 2012 after hosting acts such as the Fugees and Patti Smith, and the Bitter End, a folk music venue which opened in 1961 at 147 Bleeker St. Bob Dylan once made numerous appearances at the venue, as he launched his career.

Realizing he had reached the limitations of how far he could bring Springsteen's music career, West suggested that Springsteen sign with the New York City-based manager, Mike Appel, Santelli said. By doing so, West introduced Springsteen to his first real and professional manager, who also had connections in New York City.

"I always took my hat off to Tinker for realizing, I can't do anything more for these guys; maybe Mike can," Santelli said.

Due to Appel's persistence, Springsteen landed in a Columbia Records studio, where he auditioned for John Hammond, who had previously signed Dylan and Leonard Cohen. Springsteen impressed Hammond and signed a recording contract with the label. Attempting to make it in the music business on their own terms at the Jersey Shore, Springsteen and his bandmates in Steel Mill and The Bruce Springsteen Band had resisted heading to New York City in search of a record deal, Santelli said. Ultimately, Springsteen's trips to Greenwich Village led to his recording contract, he said. Springsteen released his first album, "Greetings from Asbury Park, N.J.," in January 1973, which was followed by "The Wild, the Innocent & the E Street Shuffle" about eight months later.

Shortly after signing the deal with Columbia Records, Springsteen called Tallent and Sancious, who were performing and living in

Josh Davidson

Richmond, and asked them to join his band. He added his former Child, Steel Mill, Bruce Springsteen Band and Dr. Zoom bandmates Lopez and Federici and started jamming with Clemons, during Jersey Shore performances with Clemons' band Norman Seldin & Joyful Noyze. Clemons performed tenor saxophone solos on "Blinded by the Light" and "Spirit in the Night," from Springsteen's debut album, and became a full-time member as Springsteen and the band prepared to tour.

The recording contract and Springsteen's decision to fill his band with Asbury Park musicians put the scene back on its feet.

Chapter 3
Swing City

"People would come over from the resorts, because they heard there was hot music going on in the west side." - Dr. Charles Horner, music historian

The vibrant music scene on Springwood Avenue spans as far back as the early 1900s. As music became an attraction inside the main hotels near the boardwalk, it also flourished in the clubs on the west side of the railroad tracks that divide the city at Springwood Avenue. The ragtime music which dominated the country in the prior decade evolved into stride piano playing and early jazz when music began on the west side at the turn of the century, Horner said. The stride piano style relies on the player's left hand keeping time with single notes and chords, with the fingers of the right hand playing separate melodic patterns, whereas ragtime focuses on syncopated rhythms.

The area's African-American community transformed Springwood Avenue into a bustling hub for music and business. Early on, the population of the west side included a diverse mixture of African-Americans, Catholics, Italians and Jews. As time progressed, African-Americans became the dominant race in the section. It wasn't long before jazz clubs, dance halls and skilled musicians filled the area, Horner said.

Asbury Park was a segregated city through the 1940s. During the decade, African-Americans were only permitted on a small portion of the beach. They were restricted from staying in local hotels and were only allowed to go to them for work, Horner said.

The Bangs Avenue Elementary School, located at 1300 Bangs Ave., was segregated until the 1950s, Horner said. The school was recently renamed the Barack H. Obama Elementary School.

"Asbury Park has a long history of being a segregated city," Horner said. "Even when segregation was eliminated legally, there was still de facto segregation and that sort of kept its residents apart to some degree. In fact, in the 1950s and 1960s, it was harder for black musicians to get jobs on the boardwalk than it was for the white musicians."

In 1913, a 14-year-old Duke Ellington and his family spent their summer vacationing in Asbury Park. Ellington, who had a job washing dishes at one of the hotels in the resort area, spent the summer closely studying piano music in the west side clubs, Horner said.

"He would go over to Springwood Avenue and listen to the music," Horner said. "He was very much influenced by it."

IN CAHOOTS, IN ASBURY PARK

Ellington's first drummer, Sonny Greer, who was born in Long Branch, started his career in Asbury Park, Horner said.

In 1922, a 17-year-old Count Basie began cutting his teeth by playing in small bands in Springwood Avenue's clubs. Shortly after, the Red Bank, New Jersey, native began playing in New York and Kansas City and went on to become a jazz legend. The famous stride pianist Fats Waller was closely associated with Asbury Park and wrote one of his most popular songs, "Honeysuckle Rose," in the home of a friend in the city in 1929, Horner said. Despite the segregation, Waller and some other African-American musicians occasionally performed at the resorts in the east side of Asbury Park, Horner said.

Many big name jazz artists were spotted visiting the west side while on tour. Many joined local musicians who would develop their chops in the clubs surrounding Springwood Avenue, before eventually earning steady gigs. In the 1940s, Springwood Avenue was a major thoroughfare for businesses, shops and clubs.

"It was fairly safe to walk around at the time," Horner said. "People would get dressed up and go to the clubs."

Mostly pop music and big bands dominated the east side during the 1940s and 1950s. Major artists like the jazz vocalist and 14-time Grammy winner Ella Fitzgerald performed in the west side, sometimes after singing at Convention Hall.

The west side had numerous large venues like The State Ballroom and Elks Club. About 1,000 Count Basie fans packed The State Ballroom when the jazz great returned to Asbury Park after making a name for himself. From the 1920s-1930s, The Royal Theater, one of the first African-American theaters in the area, hosted major entertainment, Horner said.

Patrons also found bands playing in the back of small bars and restaurants. Most of the west side's venues served alcohol. Many of the younger musicians learned from their peers, some of which took music lessons and played in their school bands, Horner said.

Jam sessions became very popular in the west side clubs during the 1940s. It was common for the musicians on stage to ask others to join them. By the 1940s and 1950s, a few dozen clubs and night spots crowded Springwood Avenue. Musicians and music fans hopped from one venue to the next, watching the music and jamming with the performers on the bill. After playing paid gigs, many musicians drifted over to the Elks Club and participated in jam sessions that ensued.

The Smile-A-While Inn, sometimes called the Smile-A-WhileCafé, began as a small hotel with a basement area, before becoming a very popular west side club. A budding but broke stride pianist and bandleader, Claude Hopkins, and his band were driving around Asbury Park in search of opportunities after losing a gig in Atlantic City. As they drove by The Smile-A-While Inn, the band heard music.

They went in and talked their way into an audition with the club's owners, who hired them to replace Basie's band. Hopkins, who had left home at the age of 21 to pursue a music career, gained great notoriety as time progressed, Horner said.

On the west side, just as many white patrons as African Americans would visit The Smile-A-While Inn, he said.

"People would come over from the resorts, because they heard there was hot music going on in the west side," Horner said.

William "Cozy" Cole, whose song "Topsy Part 2" sold more than one million copies, was born in East Orange, New Jersey, and began his career in Asbury Park. Willie Gant, a well-known jazz stride pianist and bandleader who was born in New York City, followed the same route, Horner said.

IN CAHOOTS, IN ASBURY PARK

Asbury Park's schools were integrated in the 1950s. A cross pollination of races emerged during school talent shows at Neptune High School and Asbury Park High School, where participants were both African-American and white musicians.

"So the students would get to hear different styles of music from white versus black and there was a cross fertilization," Horner said.

The emergence of rock n' roll and rhythm and blues into the mainstream spilled into Asbury Park's West side. In the 1940s, Sonny Til and The Orioles brought its rhythm and blues-styled harmonies from its home base in Baltimore to Asbury Park. The band played repeated shows in the city through the 1950s including the Asbury Park Armory, which could hold a considerable crowd. Young African-Americans from the city packed the Armory to experience performances by The Orioles and another major singing group called the Vocaliers, Horner said. The Orioles' song "It's Too Soon To Know," reached number one on the national rhythm and blues charts in 1948.

The first major rhythm and blues act that resided in Asbury Park was the Vibraneers, which was founded by Bobby Thomas in 1948. Thomas patterned the group after the nationally known Orioles. He later became a singer for the Orioles, which he had idolized. In 1954, The Vibraneers became the first Asbury Park rhythm and blues band to record an album, after cutting a few records for a small independent label in New York, Horner said.

"They were idols of everybody," Horner said. "These were fellow Asbury Park teenagers who now had a record out."

After a few of the Vibraneers' records were released, many other young vocal groups formed in Asbury Park, and patterned themselves after major rhythm and blues vocal groups. A large influx of teenaged vocal groups like The Juveniles and The Blenders played clubs on

Springwood Avenue. They were usually backed by the same jazz musicians who were already performing in the west side, Horner said.

"Though musicians might have preferences on what they wanted to play, a job is a job," he said.

The majority of the west side's small clubs in the 1950s-1960s hosted mostly African-American audiences. Larger venues, such as Cuba's, housed major artists that drew some of the white tourists who ventured into the west side to hear great music. Many white musicians who played at clubs along the boardwalk stumbled into the west side clubs where they were influenced and inspired by African-American musicians, Horner said.

"Everybody is influenced by somebody and it was common for musicians to want to see what was going on music-wise elsewhere in the city," he said.

In the west side during the 1950s, a teenaged Norman Seldin started his own booking agency, which found gigs for African-American artists in the West side clubs. He also founded one of the few record labels that existed in the area during the late 1950s and early 1960s. Many of the west side's artists were recorded on Seldin's label. The E Street Band member and west side resident Clarence Clemons played in Norman Seldin & Joyful Noyze, which Seldin booked and recorded. Gervis "Gus" Tillman, a songwriter who passed away in 1999, owned the other record label, which resided in the city at the time, Horner said. Many west side singers and groups, such as the V-Eights, Thomas and Tony Maples recorded on Tillman's Vibro record label, Horner said.

Despite the plethora of talent in the city, major labels mainly were not recording Asbury Park's music in the 1950s. Pop singer Lenny Welch, who was raised in Asbury Park, trained and developed as a singer in the west side, Horner said. He started the Marquees and spent a year singing with the Vibes in Asbury Park before moving to New York City, where he first became a nationally known recording artist. Welch's cover of "Since I Fell for You" sold more than one million copies in the early 1960s. Young singers hoping to follow in both groups' footsteps idolized their front men, Horner said.

In the 1960s, an eclectic mix of soul, rhythm and blues and jazz similar to what was heard in cities across the country became the predominant sounds in the west side, where clubs remained packed on most nights. Most of the local acts from the west side only gained recognition within the Asbury Park community. However, a fair number of artists garnered national success. Billy Brown, the lead singer of The Broadways, for example, experienced mainstream success with The Moments and Ray, Goodman & Brown.

"The Broadways were a very popular group," Horner said. "They did a couple of records for MGM."

The Broadways were backed by local musicians when the band played at smaller west side venues, such as the Orchid Lounge, he said.

"Clarence Clemons played behind The Broadways in the 1960s," Horner said. "It was a job."

Many renowned gospel groups sang in Asbury Park, where the form of music has always been alive. From 1948-1988, the Missionary Jubilaires, a major national act, sang locally and nationally, but focused mainly on storefront churches and larger religious establishments, Horner said. Gospel has greatly influenced other forms of music like jazz, blues, rhythm and blues and doo wop.

In the 1930s and 1940s, gospel was mostly sung a cappella during religious services, until the 1950s when instrumentation was added. Across the country, rhythm and blues legends like Sam Cooke and Wilson Pickett were honing their vocal craft in church before adding gospel to their interpretations of secular or non-religious music, Horner said.

Chapter 4
"Booming" in Swing City

"The jazz guys (of the west side) didn't give a shit what color you were, as long as you could play." – "Boom" Carter

Accompanied by his father at the west side clubs in 1967, the 15-year-old "Boom" Carter found himself sitting on a drum stool, from a stage surrounded by jazz legends. The Orchid Lounge became Carter's main stomping ground, where he would study the musicians' techniques. His father took photos of many of the local and national performers for *The Asbury Park Press*.

With a tiny stage that could only fit small jazz combos, the Orchid Lounge always met or exceeded its capacity of about 80 people, Carter said. The club, which attracted some of the country's greatest jazz musicians, had a house B-3 and enough space for a drum kit, bass and two or three other musicians on stage.

"Once the music started, nobody left until the end of the night," Carter said. "It was beautiful."

The club attracted the finest musicians from New York City, Newark, Philadelphia and the rest of the country, including Jimmy Smith, a Hammond B-3 organ player from Pennsylvania who infused soul and jazz into instrumental recordings which crossed over into the *Billboard* charts. Richard "Groove" Holmes, another B-3 organist, brought his experimental soul jazz to Springwood Avenue in the 1960s. Organist Jack McDuff, an organ trio bandleader who mentored and performed with George Benson, brought his soul jazz style into the Orchid Lounge. Guitarist Grant Green, from St. Louis who performed on the Blue Note Records label, performed at the Orchid Lounge, along with fellow Blue Note artist Bobby Hutcherson, who was a vibraphone and marimba player from Los Angeles, Carter said.

"The 'who's who' of jazz played at the Orchid Lounge," Carter said.

Swing players improvised until daylight neared, during jam sessions along Springwood Avenue.

"All of these great players would come through and they would take you to school," Carter said.

Being a well-known local photographer, Carter's father scored many opportunities for his son to sit in with the jazz legends on stage. The unwritten code called for musicians to ask permission before joining the band.

"My son plays drums. Do you think he can sit in?" Carter's father would ask.

"Yeah, let's see what happens," one of the performers would respond.

"It was probably a novelty for some of the people," Carter said. "A little kid playing drums with the greatest. My dad had a lot of influence."

When the band called out a familiar song, Carter would acknowledge he knew it and back them with a swing beat. If he didn't know the song, he would keep time until he could decipher its structure. Carter was born in Neptune in 1952, raised on the west side of Asbury Park and became a drummer at the age of 11. During his early years, Carter visited virtually every Springwood Avenue club.

"Up and down Springwood Avenue, every club had something good going on," Carter said.

Joe Dukes, a famous jazz drummer who held down the beat for many B-3 artists, frequented the Carter household and taught Carter valuable lessons on swing grooves and how to play behind a B-3.

"The B-3 organ is very much a part of my music and my sound," Carter said.

Dukes and other jazz legends sat with Carter at his drums and imparted their wealth of knowledge to him. Some played his father's keyboard or old, beat up guitar. Dukes had dinner with the Carter family each time he visited.

"He would sit down and show me a lot of stuff," Carter said. "I learned a lot from Joe Dukes. He's gone now, but he was a tough guy."

Born in Memphis, Dukes died in December of 1992. He was 55.

Jealousy was a non-factor in the west side music scene, where the musicians looked out for one another, Carter said.

"Everybody was just trying to make music and have fun with it," Carter said.

Carter's early mentors crammed swing's most critical fundamentals into his young brain. Carter learned that as a drummer, he would be responsible for keeping the groove together.

"Everybody has to keep time, but drums stand out more as a beat, so time is very prominent, it's right there," Carter said. "If you slow down or speed up, it's very noticeable."

IN CAHOOTS, IN ASBURY PARK

Guitarists and keyboardists can stagger beats during solos, but the drummer's job is to keep time, hold the groove and synchronize the entire band's sound, he said.

"The main thing is the groove and it's the drummer's job to lock down that time," Carter said.

Recognizing the younger drummer's tendency to play each song at a faster than necessary pace, the older players made every attempt to slow him down. Playing tasteful means less is more, he learned. The older musicians instilled in him the discipline necessary to play for the song.

"When you're that young, you try to play a little faster than what it calls for, because you have so much energy," he said. "Once they calmed that down in me, I kind of got it."

They also showed him how to lock himself into a swing groove and focus on his bandmates. They showed him how to maintain the important structural components of each song, during improvised sections.

"Certain things are set in stone with jazz," he said.

Carter learned which aspects of his drumming needed the most work and the importance of all musicians maintaining a strict practice regimen, regardless of their talent.

With a young, creative mind open to new ideas, Carter firmly fixed his ears on the live music inside the Orchid Lounge. He studied the musicians intently, before spending countless hours at home turning their styles and techniques into his own.

"These guys were doing things that I couldn't even imagine," Carter said. "It was such a beautiful vibe there. It was all about the music."

The music of Springwood Avenue is alive in Carter's music today, along with any of the music that inspired him throughout his career. Carter has developed an eclectic taste in music, playing many styles including rock, jazz and blues.

"I always respect the ones who came before me and helped me and the ones I have always respected as musicians," he said.

Playing the drums was a source of enjoyment for Carter; so much so, that he would practice in his parents' basement for 11 hours a day.

"I would come out and the time would go by so fast, because I was having fun," Carter said. "That's what happens every time I sit down and play; I think about those days in the basement of my parent's house. That's my mantra. I remember that and it keeps me going today."

On the west side, Carter first played in many soul bands including Hot Ice. In high school, his daily routine included going to school, working at a local music store, playing gigs and repeating the process.

"It's been music all of my life, just about," he said.

People came from New York and other East Coast cities to experience the unbelievable music scene of Asbury Park's west side.

"It was just a beautiful time," Carter said. "Everybody was just working their butts off trying to get something done."

Carter said that his parents were part of a large community of adults who worked hard to support their children. Racial tension existed underneath the emotional surface, but didn't reach its boiling point until the riots of July 1970, he said. Carter was 8 when he first experienced racism. Traveling in the southern United States, the frustrated child questioned why he could not use a "whites only" bathroom. His father grabbed him abruptly and brought him down the road to urinate in the bushes.

"The first time I went down South, I was totally unware of how racist it was down there, compared to where I was growing up in Asbury," he said. "I didn't understand it until it was explained to me, because we had such a beautiful life growing up."

As he grew older, Carter experienced the reality of the racism inflicted upon the United States and the east side of the Springwood Avenue railroad tracks in Asbury Park. Bigotry struck closer to home when he was 11. An excited Carter and his friend were invited to swim in the astounding pool at the Berkley-Carteret Hotel, across the street from Convention Hall. Shortly after arriving, they were told their skin color would prohibit them from swimming. Seeing their white friends swimming in front of them, the two boys couldn't comprehend why they were thrown out of the pool.

During early morning walks on the soft sand of the Asbury beach with his dog, Carter would suddenly hear, "Hey you, get off the beach! You're not allowed on this part of the beach!"

Carter's final two years of high school were marred by racial tension. One white history teacher's disdain sent Carter to summer school after his senior year.

"I failed, or so she said," Carter said. "I thought I did well, but either way I had to go to summer school and that kind of pissed me off."

Some of his white high school teachers were racist, and some African-American teachers became fed up at how they were being treated by whites.

"They didn't know who to hate or who to take it out on, so they took it out on the students," Carter said.

But other teachers of all colors and races took extra steps to guide their students to a better life, Carter said. Seeing the potential young students like Carter had, they helped them plan ahead to achieve their goals.

Some of the negative teachers successfully obstructed their students' paths to success. When Carter sought a spot in the high school band, his guidance counselor steered him toward a new vocational school where students could learn trades, such as cooking or machinery. As the two discussed Carter's post-graduation plans, Carter told the guidance counselor he wanted to be a musician. Joining the high school band would help Carter refine his musical skills and learn to read music.

Needing to fulfil a quota of students required to start the vocational school, the guidance counselor told Carter he would be going to the vocational school rather than joining band.

"So, I became a machinist," Carter said.

After graduating high school, Carter came home from his job as a machinist at a factory near Main Street, his body covered in grease and metal chips wedged in his arms. Safety for factory workers was not a factor at the time. Workers wore safety goggles, but no arm protection, Carter said.

"I could have been impaled doing that job," he said. "I did it for six months and made some good money. Next thing you know, I went on the road (as a musician) and never looked back. I never went back to that job again."

Carter still respects the trade, understanding that machinists have built and designed the drum pedals he uses today.

Music has always been Carter's escape from the stress that surfaces throughout the day. From the drum stool in the basement of his parent's house through his final high school years, Carter released some tension by learning the latest Santana or Chicago albums either by himself or with other musicians. Music provided solace during the six months he spent as a machinist.

"After anything bothered me from work, I played for a few hours and I was in heaven," Carter said. "It was such a spiritual, uplifting thing to sit down, sweat and play."

Growing up, Carter and his friends spent up to six hours a day listening to music. Music integrated young teenagers from diverse races who may have never become friends. His life was always consumed by playing and listening to music. As the teenaged Carter grew older, he

IN CAHOOTS, IN ASBURY PARK

snuck across the train tracks to east side clubs like The Upstage, Fast Lane and Sunshine Inn. He jammed with other musicians underneath a church on 4th Avenue, which bared an odd resemblance to The Upstage, Day-Glo paint and all.

Carter frequented The Upstage with his father even before he began to play in the club. Tom Potter was friends with Carter's father and visited his photography studio on many occasions. One day, Potter invited his father to The Upstage to view some photos in the club. Tom and Margaret Potter both made frequent visits to the Carter photography studio to see Joseph Carter and his wife.

"They were nice people and were down to Earth, just like my dad," Carter said. "They respected my father and my father respected them."

After visiting with his father, Carter returned to The Upstage on his own and joined some of the jam sessions inside. Inside the venue, he met and formed a lifelong bond with a young Sancious, who played keyboard and guitar. Sancious, who was an original member of The E Street Band, played keyboards on Springsteen's debut "Greetings from Asbury Park, N.J." (Columbia: 1973) and sophomore effort "The Wild the Innocent & the E Street Shuffle" (Columbia: 1973). In 1975, Carter and Sancious were the drummer and keyboardist respectively on the title track of Springsteen's "Born to Run" album (Columbia: 1975). During his career, Sancious has also performed with Sting, Eric Clapton, Jeff Beck, Peter Gabriel and Seal.

Carter made repeated trips to The Upstage to watch his high school friends perform and to experience the world inside. Boom's father wasn't a huge fan of his son hanging out at the Upstage. One night when Boom didn't come home on time, Joseph Carter searched for him at The Upstage. Recognizing the unlikeness of his 5'8" father finding him in the dark, crowded club, Boom quickly made a "beeline" for the exit.

"I was there, but I had an escape route," the younger Carter said. "I figured out how to get out the back door, so I ducked out on him."

Though jealousy affected some musicians, Carter only surrounded himself with artists whose sole focus was creating music.

"To me everybody was trying to do the same thing: develop their craft and have some fun doing it," Carter said.

Females were a motivator for Carter, who found himself playing harder and faster to impress them. He learned quickly that he couldn't win over all of them, as some would have a preference for the style of his counterparts.

"Women had a big part in how hard you played and how hard you wanted to push it, because everyone knew, if the band sounded good, you were going to bring some girls in," Carter said.

Sometimes, Boom and his friends hung out with the area's rich white kids, since they could afford all of the "cooler" musical instruments, such as the brand name gear used by The Doors.

"You had to have some money to buy that stuff," Carter said. "They had a little more money."

Carter's eclectic musical taste and open mind made it easy for him to adjust when he crossed the tracks and played rock n' roll on Asbury's east side. In an effort to spread their disdain for the Caucasian race, some of Carter's friends tried unsuccessfully to steer him away from white music. White teenagers discouraged their friends from listening to jazz, due to its influence by African-Americans, Carter said. With positive encouragement from his west side mentors, Carter didn't discriminate between the jazz styles of John Coltrane or Jeff Beck.

"The jazz guys (of the west side) didn't give a shit what color you were, as long as you could play," Carter said.

The jazz bands led by Ellington and Basie both included a talented mixture of African-American and white musicians, he said.

IN CAHOOTS, IN ASBURY PARK

"I think musicians broke down many of the walls for a lot of racial problems," Carter said.

In his household, Carter's family played records of virtually every musical style from country, Motown, rock, gospel, jazz and blues. One day, as Boom waited for Joseph Carter to call him downstairs and drive him to school, Boom was mesmerized by what he had heard on the FM radio.

"All of the sudden, I heard this sound come on and I was like, what the fuck is that?" he said.

He made it halfway through the song, before his dad yelled for him to come downstairs. Still astonished and curious to find out who the artist was, Boom headed to school with his father. That afternoon he ran home from school, dropped his books in his room, turned on the radio and waited for the sound to reemerge. Finally, he was equally stunned by another song from the same artist.

"It was The Jimi Hendrix Experience," Carter said.

So he went downtown to a local record store, looking for Hendrix's music. Shuffling through the bins, he stumbled upon a record with a fisheye lens photo of the band on the cover and a warning that the listener would experience something they had never heard on the back. Released in August 1967, Hendrix's debut album, "Are You Experienced?" (Reprise Records) had a profound impact on the young drummer.

"I must have played it over and over and over and I can go on," Carter said. "I had to buy another one eventually."

It was his first self-purchased contribution to the Carter household's extensive record collection.

"I brought that in the house and everybody was like, 'What the freak is that? That's not music. What are you listening to?'" Carter said.

So he played the first single, "Purple Haze," for his friends, but failed to win them over.

"What the hell is that stuff, man, take that off," said a friend, who made him put on a Temptations album.

It took a little more than a year until Carter gained respect for bringing Hendrix into Asbury Park's African-American community. In October 1968, Hendrix released the album "Electric Ladyland" (Reprise), which featured the soulful ballad, "Have You Ever Been (To Electric Ladyland)."

One day, Carter's friends walked down to his basement, where he was listening to the song.

"Oh shit, man, who's that guy?" they said.

His friends reverted to their original attitudes when the next song, a raucous, squealing rocker called "Crosstown Traffic," blasted across the room.

"What the hell is that?" they said, as Carter explained that it was written and recorded by the same artist.

"Their minds weren't open to something outside of the norm," he said.

Hendrix opened up Carter's musical journey to a completely different style of music. He soon found himself listening to Led Zeppelin, Cream and Jeff Beck, but still struggled to turn his friends on to his new discoveries.

"They just wouldn't get into it, because it was just a bunch of white boys doing it," Carter said.

After Hendrix's post-death recognition, Carter's friends were eager learn more about the artist who by then had attained worldwide respect. They began asking Carter for details of Hendrix's history. Carter set the goal of playing with Hendrix, on the day he first heard him. Hendrix's death marked the end of his dream.

IN CAHOOTS, IN ASBURY PARK

"Then my brother David Sancious came along, picked up the guitar and I said, Oh, there it is, I don't need Hendrix anymore. David can do this stuff. He can play like that. I can play drums behind what he's doing," Carter said. "We were friends ever since."

At the time, Sancious, whose mother was a classically trained musician, was listening to Hendrix, Cream and a lot of jazz, Carter said.

"David had the open mindedness I was looking for and he had it in abundance – he was a freaking genius," Carter said. "David was my friend, my partner in music and also my teacher. He's a year younger than me, but the kid was so advanced."

Sancious taught Carter how to play odd-metered timings and expanded his horizons to playing and writing on the guitar.

"He taught me how to be creative and about being unafraid to try out what I was hearing in my head," Carter said. "If you can hum it, then you can probably play it."

By encouraging Carter to play different meters in various time signatures, Sancious pushed Carter to sail across unchartered waters. With some practice, playing in odd-meters became second nature for Carter.

"Once you figure it out, you build a pulse just like anything else," Carter said. "But without him, I don't think I would ever have learned that stuff."

One night, with a guitar case in his hand, Sancious walked into the Student Prince on Kingsley Street as Matthews and his friend Annie Furloung danced to the Bank Street Blues Band, which featured Lyon on harmonica.

"He got up on stage and it was like Jimi Hendrix entered the room," Matthews said. "Dave is an amazing musician. He may actually be the best one to come out of the scene. Dave was something special."

Chapter 5
A Drop of the Psychedelic

"In '67 and '68, the 'greasers' were trying to beat us up and they were all drinking their Colt 45. By '69 or '70, they were looking to buy some stuff from us." – Tom Matthews, music fan

Growing up as next door neighbors in Belmar, Luraschi and Sancious, a pair of close friends who were bonded by their passion for music, took many trips to The Upstage via bicycle and bus.

"David was very talented," Luraschi said.

Luraschi eventually replaced the bicycle with a motorcycle for trips to the club where he also met Springsteen and all of the original E Street Band members, along with Kenn and Southside Johnny.

As a teenager, Luraschi chained his bike to a rack outside of The Upstage, entered through the front door and closely observed the playing and performing techniques of those who were older and established in

IN CAHOOTS, IN ASBURY PARK

the scene like Billy Ryan, who played "The Circuit" as lead guitarist for The Jaywalkers. The older musicians made about $400-500 week, a more than modest salary in 1968, and impressed their younger counterparts when they drove past them in fancy cars with beautiful women in the passenger's seats.

"Life was sweet for them," Luraschi said. "They were what was happening. If they asked you to play, you would be thrilled."

One day, while sitting on his bicycle inside The Upstage, Luraschi stuck up a conversation with local musician Harry London

"I really like your band" he told London.

"What, do you play?" London replied.

Luraschi told London that he did and found himself on stage jamming on a song during the next set.

"I thought that was really neat," said Luraschi, during an interview in front of the former Upstage in 2002. "We still talk about that when I see him from time to time."

Upon opening in 1968, The Upstage struggled to gain popularity. After word spread of a new place to jam after the other bars closed, the venue became the final nightly stop for many musicians and their fans. Live music constantly pumped through its speakers in the form of long jam sessions. The area's best musicians vamped on songs by The Animals, Cream, rhythm and blues, early blues rock and Hendrix, whose music had just reached the mainstream radio.

"It got to be the place to go after the other bars closed; it was really something," Luraschi said. "They would come from near and far."

The Upstage was surrounded by a swarm of local businesses and shops. Many closed by sundown and Asbury became a bar town by 9 p.m. each night. Before shopping malls were built in Monmouth County, Cookman Avenue bustled with shoppers who came from locations throughout the state and visited Steinbach's department store. Reporters filed their stories at *The Asbury Park Press* headquarters building, which also existed on the avenue.

The Upstage Club and Green Mermaid Café were the sole bars owned by the Potters, who were very supportive of the local music scene. They lived nearby on Cookman Avenue, where they owned the nearby Romeo's Landing, where Margaret worked as a hair stylist during the day. The Potters were inspired to open the venue after their living room had become crowded with musicians who came over to jam, Matthews said. So Tom Potter purchased the warehouse space above the

first floor's Thom McAn shoe store. The second floor housed the Green Mermaid Café where Margaret's band, Margaret and the Distractions, began a typical night at 9 p.m.

The Green Mermaid in the late 1960s. (Photo courtesy of Ed Mueller)

Each night, the Upstage closed for 30 minutes, following a more than three hour early set that ended at midnight. Patrons who were older than 17 were permitted to re-enter the club at 12:30 a.m. for the late set on the third floor, which ended after a maximum of three and a half hours.

Zoning laws had legally restricted the younger patrons from entering after midnight and enjoying the free form jamming that ensued.

Musicians jam at the venue in the late 1960s.
(Photos courtesy of Ed Mueller)

About a dozen musicians graced the venue's stage on a typical night to join the legendary sessions, led by Margaret Potter, Luraschi said. Many musicians came to the club after finishing their set at nearby venues.

"They would play all night long," Luraschi said. "People would come from all over."

The Upstage's largest rooms reached 120 feet in length. Though one might think the low ceilings would produce a poor live sound, the result was contrary, Matthews said. However, recorded music didn't fare as well.

"There was a recording that was out from the Upstage and it was like, what is this garbage?'" Amato said.

As surrounding bars closed for the night, patrons extended their night of partying at The Upstage, which had no legal closing time, since alcohol was not served inside, Luraschi said. The club became filled with music aficionados who drank coffee and enjoyed live acoustic music on the second floor's Green Mermaid Cafe, before heading upstairs to observe Asbury's finest musicians collaborate on stage. The venue's inner décor bared a close resemblance to some of the Nation's hippest clubs. Tom Potter designed the entire interior on his own, enlisting the help of volunteers rather than hiring carpenters, Luraschi said.

"I would come in if I had a day off and help him wire stuff up," Luraschi said. "He would scrounge speakers and amplifiers from all over. It was a real mom and pop operation, but it was cool."

Potter punched huge holes into the black, Day-Glo-covered drywall to the side of the stage, which housed built-in PA speakers. Musicians also had their choice between the many amplifiers built into the counter at the front of the stage, Luraschi said. If the amp worked, it would become the musician's gear for the night. A small collection of stage monitors allowed musicians to hear the activity on stage.

IN CAHOOTS, IN ASBURY PARK

A Day-Glo image from the venue in the late 1970s.
(Photos courtesy of Ed Mueller)

The Upstage was one of a few Asbury Park clubs with the Day-Glo theme. Many of its murals were created by Tom Potter with other decorations added by additional Asbury Park artists. Other clubs like New York's Café Wha?, the legendary former CBGB club and some venues in San Francisco had similar Day-Glo styles of design, but the "speaker-in-the-wall concept" developed at The Upstage was unprecedented in the late 1960s-early 1970s, Luraschi said.

Tom Potter and his artist friends painted many of the decorative, thematic displays directly onto the walls of the venue. They created abstract art in Day-Glo paint, which stood out over the club's pitch black walls. They also attached large objects to the walls, which included spray painted mannequins surrounded by black lights. Artwork was always augmented and never removed from the collection, leaving no space uncovered.

The Day-Glo theme that saturated the Upstage was inspired by drug use, but the venue's straight-minded owners did everything they could to keep drugs out of the venue. Drug use was common outside of the club, but Tom Potter did not allow narcotics inside. Leaving the club and returning was prohibited to prevent patrons from coming in high after smoking pot in the alley. Some still managed to do so, but most people were scared to take drugs in open locations at the time, Matthews said.

Fights were a rare occurrence inside the club, though some sketchy activity occurred in its surrounding vicinity.

"People were always usually too high to get into fights," Matthews said.

Luraschi's brother, Eddie, a bouncer at the club, always kept an eye on his sibling's well-being. The other gladiator-sized bouncers, which included Bobby Williams, John Nicholson and Danny Gallagher, were so large that they all had the word "Big" added in front of their legal names.

"They were all 6'6", 300 pounders," Luraschi said.

"Big Bobby" Williams was an accomplished Asbury Park drummer who played with Van Zandt, Tallent and Southside Johnny in Funky Dusty and the Soul Broom Band. He also played in Dr. Zoom and the Sonic Boom.

"He would lay it down," said Luraschi of Williams. "He would huff and puff and sweat, but he would play."

Matthews recalled a performance by one of Williams' bands at the Sunshine Inn. The band, which was an offshoot of Steel Mill, played straight ahead rock, with some rhythm and blues. Williams played the drums in a way that was audibly and visually noticeable to the audience, Matthews recalled.

"They were really good," he said.

In January 2000, Williams died at the age of 52.

By the late 1960s, Springsteen was established on top of Asbury Park's musical hierarchy, Santelli said. Once successful, Springsteen and Van Zandt had a strong influence over which musicians were allowed to jam at The Upstage, Santelli said. Ultimately, the Potters determined the pecking order of either skilled musicians who wanted to maintain their chops and see how they compared to other players or the marginal ones who just wanted to get on stage.

While walking home from Asbury Park to Belmar on many nights in the late 1960s, Luraschi would recall what he witnessed inside The Upstage. He frequently shared his disbelief with a passerby, shouting across the boardwalk.

"Holy shit, what was that, man?" he would yell.

The conversation would continue about a young Springsteen jumping on stage and electrifying the club's top floor with a rendition of a popular tune, such as "Soul Man."

Even then, Luraschi struggled to put his finger on the greatness that emerged before his eyes.

"That kid was always good," Luraschi said. "Even when he was a kid, he was good. I always saw something different in him, then. He had an inner light inside of him – he had it."

The skinny yet ambitious musician, who is now known around the world as "The Boss," let nothing stand in the way of his success. He sought out any and every opportunity to perform.

"He wanted it more than a lot of dudes," Luraschi said. "He had to try harder than everyone else. He had a lot of stuff going against him."

Springsteen focused solely on playing music. Any side attractions, such as money, were just part of the landscape available for those who declined to commit their lives to performing. Springsteen thrived with talent, drive and persistence. With bare pockets and armed with charisma, character and skill, Springsteen soon turned any non-believers into fans, Luraschi said.

"He had nothing to offer," Luraschi said. "He had a pocket full of dreams, but no money."

Josh Davidson

Inside The Upstage, the spotlight only shined for those brave and courageous enough to put their material needs aside, step on the gas and bring their dreams to life. Asbury Park's musicians bonded even during the toughest of times. Barely a moment went by without the hysterical laughter and memories that were etched in the minds of those who were part of the scene.

"I know when it's time for me to go, if I sit back when I'm old, I am just going to sit there and cry and laugh so hard," Luraschi said. "I will laugh until I cry."

Luraschi died of lung cancer in 2009.

In 1969, a 17-year-old Santelli played with a separate set of musicians in a scene that developed in and around the Jersey Shore borough of Bay Head. At The Upstage, Springsteen, Sancious and Van Zandt captivated his attention the most. Springsteen organized many of the jams and guided his counterparts through magical sets on stage.

"They would cover Cream and Hendrix and do all of this blues stuff," Santelli said. "It was pretty amazing to watch it."

Sancious stood out because he was one of a few African-Americans who jammed in The Upstage, but more for his tremendous guitar playing ability, Santelli said. Racial tension between Caucasians and African-Americans in the city prevented young African-Americans from entering The Upstage.

"My God, he could play," Santelli said. "He struck me as similar to a young Jimi Hendrix."

Van Zandt also played a major role in the club.

"He had this endless energy and he was someone who seemed to be everywhere at once on stage," Santelli said.

As they watched the three musicians from the audience, Santelli and his friends each felt like hanging up their guitars for good. Without a license or money to buy a car, Santelli looked up to the three musicians, who were a couple of years older and had established themselves as musicians.

"They were just so much better than anything that was happening in the Point Pleasant Beach or Bay Head area," he said.

Matthews' first trip to the venue had an immediate impact. Anne Furloung, who had already frequented the venue, first dragged Matthews to the club when he was 15.

Starting at 3rd from left, Tom Matthews, Katie Ferris, Anne Furloung, "George," Billy Connelley, Nancy Ferris and "Pepsi" at the Green Mermaid in the late 1960s. (Photo courtesy of Ed Mueller)

"I had been sent away to the Diagnostic Center for a while in 1968," Matthews said. "I got out in January of 1969 and she said, 'oh man, you've got to come check this place out, so she dragged me down there.'

"It was pretty amazing," he said. "It was like a little bit of the big city psychedelic scene had come to Asbury. Before that, we were reading about it in *Time* magazine. Now, we had a piece of it in our town. It was like a little bit of San Francisco, dropped into Asbury Park."

He immediately returned to the club and attempted to sneak his way up to the third floor.

To this day, Matthews vividly recalls the diverse mix of personalities that existed on the boardwalk and in the clubs of Asbury Park in the 1960s, just as it transitioned from a tourist habitat to a predominantly rock n' roll music scene. Within the city' borders were the hippies who had long hair, multi-patterned, colorful clothing and short-syllabled vernacular. There were the outcasts to the rest of city known as the "freaks," whose dress, appearance and verbiage veered from the norm. Holdovers from the 1950s, the "greasers" looked as if they were pulled straight out of "The West Side Story" movie. They spared no expense and donned knitted shirts, leather jackets and pointy shoes, Matthews recalled.

"In '67 and '68, the 'greasers' were trying to beat us up and they were all drinking their Colt 45. By '69 or '70, they were looking to buy some stuff from us," Matthews said. "Their hair was getting longer."

Asbury Park's "collegians" were the serious types who put their heads down, and their energy forward on their school work. They avoided the drugs, excessive alcohol and the late night temptations of the city.

For Matthews, Asbury Park of the late-1960s still had the look and feel of a carnival. It had all of the elements: sugary and greasy food, swarms of people, circus rides and debauchery before and through the night. The Upstage was its eclectic mecca, where the audience became part of the show. The Upstage was Asbury Park's hippie headquarters, and became a second home to all types of people who either were part of the show or flies on the wall.

A habitual class cutter, Matthews finally dropped out of the ninth grade on his 16th birthday in 1970. When Matthews didn't meet the venue's age limit, he did manage a dozen times to sneak past the bouncers with a gaggle of distracting young girls, to the club's third floor jam sessions. The third floor was always packed, but the scene down below was either filled or empty on a given night. The diverse mix of people, many times, developed into a sideshow off stage.

"There were a lot of people who kind of fit and others who had come to see the spectacle," Matthews said. "We were part of the show, I think."

Audiences came from a variety of walks of life. Some walked straight and narrow paths to see what the buzz was about at The Upstage. Others, who had stumbled along crooked paths, arrived at The Upstage and fit right in. Inside its doors, each person was a walking novel, whose stories began with their brightly colored wardrobes, which sometimes camouflaged them into the spectrum of colors on the club's walls and stairs. Many competed to look and act the oddest, Matthews said.

On the boardwalk, some young girls bought ice cream and kept the spoons, so they could whack band members like Springsteen and Van Zandt in the butt with them. The girls thought the act would transform the spoons into precious artifacts of the future, Matthews said.

By providing music at the Green Mermaid Café, the Potters opened its doors to all teenagers hoping to experience the club. The Upstage never made the Potters rich; instead, it fed the musical passion both they and thousands of music fans possessed. Tom Potter was a character in his own right, known for his enormous leather belt, with an eight-inch wide belt buckle. The Upstage made the Potters known throughout the area, Amato said. Amato and Matthews were still too young to visit many bars until the drinking age dropped from 21 to 18 in 1972.

"They made a name for themselves by running that club," he said.

The Potters spent most of their time at the club, where The Distractions could be found mostly at the Green Mermaid Café, playing early rock covers.

"(The Distractions) weren't as good as the big jams taking place upstairs, but they were pretty cool," Matthews said.

The Potters provided the musicians with mentorship, opportunities to perform, as well food, space to practice and sleep and anything else they needed to excel in their young careers, Santelli said.

"They were the mom and the pop of the scene," he said. "They were nurturing and encouraging, but they didn't have that incredible business sense that was necessary to make the jump from Asbury Park to the bigtime in New York City."

At the time, talented musicians from East Coast states such as Delaware, Connecticut or New Jersey traveled to Greenwich Village for a chance to further their careers by performing in the brighter lights of the city. Artist and repertoire representatives from major labels never scoured the Jersey Shore in search of the next big thing. They discovered them in The Village. The Potters recognized the immense talent in the Asbury Park music scene, which never translated into a record deal, Santelli said.

"Nurturing was what they did and they did it very, very well," Santelli said. "They were absolutely essential to the scene."

Growing up in troubled homes where they were rejected by their parents for having long hair, being hippies and playing music, many teenagers found solace at The Upstage, he said.

"They found a home away from home with mom and pop Potter," Santelli said. Surrounding live music bars in Asbury Park, such as Steve Brody's, Magic Touch and Mrs. Jay's, closed two or three hours earlier than the Upstage. After performing at those bars, cover bands finished the night by jamming at the Upstage before it closed at 5 a.m. Inside, they joined the refreshingly free form jams, after playing verbatim versions of top 40 music at the other establishments.

"Come 3 o'clock and they would just go and get their little amplifiers and run over to The Upstage to play because then they could jam, they could play what they wanted," Amato said.

The Upstage was a melting pot for budding Jersey Shore instrumentalists and vocalists to develop into musicians, Amato said. Like the Cavern Club in Liverpool, England, and Haight-Ashbury in San Francisco, Asbury Park was on a short list of music scenes in that period, Matthews said.

The Potters paid close attention to the quality of music in The Upstage and sent bands that hadn't polished their chops off stage.

"If you weren't good, you weren't on," Amato said.

The 13-year-old Billy Hector learned this the hard way when he walked into The Upstage with his guitar during a family trip to the Jersey Shore in 1968. Hector was nervous and surrounded by musicians who were five years his senior and much more experienced. Unlike Springsteen who created a buzz in the venue, Hector might as well have been a ghost.

"When you're 13 and the other musicians are like 18 or 19, you don't even rate," he said.

Hector's cousin landed both young men a gig at the Green Mermaid Café after meeting

Margaret Potter outside of the Thom McAn shoe store, at the ground level of the building.

"We played there and we weren't really that good," Hector said.

Hector was in the process of teaching his cousin, who lived in a summer home next door to his family's, how to play bass, since he didn't know any other musicians in Asbury Park. Without owning an actual bass guitar, Hector down-tuned one of his six string electric guitars, so his cousin could emulate the instrument.

During the performance, Hector heard Tom Potter yell a stern warning from the audience: "Stop farting around and play some music or else we're throwing you out of here."

"That scared the shit out of us, because he was a big, cartoon character kind of a guy," Hector said. "We were just kids."

Hector's other cousins sat in the front row cheering as the "stink fest" ensued. One young musician, who Hector could not identify at the time, did encourage the band, by giving them a thumbs up. Since he remembers a girl saying the person was a good guitar player, Hector believes it was either local guitar whiz Rick DeSarno or Springsteen.

"Who knows who it was, I have no idea," Hector said. "It could have been Southside.

It could have been Ricky D. It could have been anybody."

After playing at the venue, a frightened Hector made an abrupt exit without meeting any of the local musicians. He headed straight home, armed with the knowledge that, "I had to really get my shit together."

"I was really very scared," Hector said. "I went home. It was a real learning experience, because we really sucked. I knew we did. And I went home feeling very bad."

Hector's first trip to The Upstage became his last.

"I just got my shit together somewhere else," he said. "I would have to really, really have it together to go back, because I thought I really, really sucked. I wasn't a phenom."

Following his experience at The Upstage, Hector persevered and intensely practiced the guitar at his family's summer home in neighboring Ocean Grove.

IN CAHOOTS, IN ASBURY PARK

"I stopped going to the beach," Hector said. "I just wanted to play guitar and there was a piano in the house, so I was playing that all the time too. I got the calling and I didn't want to do anything else."

The 13-year-old focused on learning the guitar's minute intricacies, years before becoming an Asbury Park Music Awards Living Legend. It took a few more years for a skilled rock guitar player to move to his neighborhood in Orange, New Jersey. The new neighbor gave Hector the daily opportunity to learn the language of rock firsthand, instead of gaining exposure from a guitarist standing 150 feet away from him at a rock concert.

"There were no real guitar magazines or things like that," Hector said. "It was all like a mystery, even to the guitar teachers that I went to. They didn't really understand what was happening in rock. They understood what was happening in jazz and what Les Paul was doing, but not Eric Clapton."

When he wasn't intensely honing his guitar chops during the summer visits to Asbury Park as a child, Hector strolled the boardwalk, and usually headed north from Ocean Grove to the corner of Ocean and Second Avenues, where The Stone Pony now sits. At the time, a venue called The Blue Grotto existed in same building. Hector would walk next door to a shop called Poster Freak. Inside was a large warehouse filled with black light posters. Since the posters were a new phenomenon, patrons had to pay 50 cents just to go in a room and view black light posters under a strobe light. The Pharaohs, a popular band, played nearby at car shows and bars such as Steve Brody's.

With wooden planks at his feet, Hector experienced the sights and sounds of the carnival disguised as a boardwalk. He would hear the Salvation Army Band playing "Spirit in the Sky," as the voices of the auctioneers and shoppers, who bartered loudly, saturated the Ocean Avenue breeze.

"The boardwalk was a real show back then," Hector said.

Matthews had left Asbury Park with his girlfriend and was in Toronto when he saw Asbury Park in flames on the cover of the *New York Times* during the riots of July 1970. About one week later, he returned to the city and discovered that The Upstage's contingent of fans had multiplied. An enormous group of hippies had migrated from Greenwich Village to Asbury Park, where they slept beneath the casino boardwalk and at the Monte Carlo building, until the police appeared in riot gear and cleared the location, Matthews said. With only the money that had already accumulated in their pockets, the hippies from the Village had intended to take the bus or train south to the beach. They landed in Asbury Park.

"Our little scene that was maybe 20 or 30 people, was now 150," he said. "1970 was when the whole thing kind of coalesced in Asbury, around early July, near the time of the riots. A lot of people came down from the Village and just stayed and that kind of built the scene a little bit."

For a short period of time in the early 1970s, the music scene grew as the rest of the city began to decay.

The Upstage has not reopened since it closed in 1971, but many of its past musicians have returned to tour the vacant inside. Surprisingly, most of the Day-Glo paint from the late 1960s still lines The Upstage's walls today.

Some interest has been reported of developers seeking to purchase and renovate The Upstage. An individual once purchased the venue with the intention of reopening it as a museum where patrons can experience its history, Gilmour said. Gilmour speculated that the owner would have held a limited number of concerts in the venue. The owner underestimated the expense of renovating the space, which is now up for sale again, Gilmour said. The stringent city building codes that exist today would require expensive renovations for the space. The Americans with

IN CAHOOTS, IN ASBURY PARK

Disability Act requirements would most certainly require the installation of a very expensive elevator so handicapped individuals could access the third floor, Gilmour said. There is a chance that a new developer will purchase the space and turn it into condos, but the high asking price might discourage that from taking place, he said.

"I don't know what's going to happen with it to tell you the truth," he said.

Chapter 6
High Times in Psychedelic City

"There are the lucky ones who have done it and stopped, but there are the other ones who had that habitual 'can't quit the shit' and they took it to extremes. It screws up your music. It screwed up their lives." –
"Boccigalupe"

As snow fell during New Years shows at The Upstage and The Sunshine Inn, Matthews experienced the irony of taking white acid. "That was nice," he recalled while laughing. "It was kind of a theme. Everything was white."

The Asbury Park crowd of the early 1970s sampled a wide variety of drugs and acid was one of the favorites. Crack cocaine didn't exist, while powdered cocaine was only snorted on occasion. On rare occasions Matthews, who mainly stuck to acid, would experiment with heroin. At one point, he and a small group of friends had a heroin and eggs breakfast.

Until the mid-1970s drugs such as hallucinogens, uppers, downers and pot were predominant. They were benign in comparison to the powered drugs, including cocaine, speed and heroin, which were Asbury Park's elite illegal substances from 1976-1977. While many musicians could keep up with the band while under the influence of cocaine, the same couldn't be said for those on heroin or Dilaudids, Amato said. There were some exceptions who could take a major drug without their bandmates or peers noticing. In general, hallucinogenic drugs didn't have the life-altering or lethal effects of powders such as heroin and cocaine, Amato said. Experimenting users mixed separate narcotics together for increased potency.

"Everything was about experimentation," Amato said. "The drugs were experimentation; the music was experimentation; everything was experimentation. Sometimes it got a little too far."

Since Amato and Matthews grew up in Asbury Park, their parents had ties to the city's police and judges, which diminished their chances of a drug-related arrest.

Club patrons and musicians, like Amato, stood in the back room of a building, where they examined little sheets of paper under a black light. The paper had a small picture of Snoopy and his dog house. If tiny dots appeared on the picture, the buyer knew that the sheet contained lysergic acid diethylamide (LSD). If they didn't, he or she was being duped out of the $2 to $5 they spent on getting high for the night.

One of Amato's acquaintances, who was going to school in Florida, met a classmate who self-manufactured sheets of paper sprinkled with LSD on a picture. Amato's acquaintance would mail them up the east coast to friends for their recreational drug use. Technology didn't exist in the early 1970s to scan envelopes for illegal substances.

Josh Davidson

Though living on modest incomes, the members of the Asbury Park community always managed to get drugs. Generous users shared them.

"There always seemed to be enough money for that," Matthews said.

During the Vietnam War era, hallucinogenic drug use increased throughout the country. By 1969, more than 500,000 members of the U.S. armed forces were involved in the war, which bitterly divided citizens across the country, causing sometimes fatal domestic protests. Protests of the Vietnam War were common in Asbury Park, but violence rarely occurred as a result.

"We all knew the cops and they knew us," Matthews said. "It was kind of like, 'Oh God, you guys again,' during the protests."

One officer, James Cooke, who they called "Cookie," used to greet throngs of partiers at the door of his friend's house in Ocean Grove. Matthews and his friends laughed, as Cooke stood in his uniform, freaking out many of the partiers.

When the police showed up to confiscate their drugs, Matthews and his friends showed them how to identify latest narcotics, so they knew what to look for during other busts. Though he and his friends were arrested as they became older, their juvenile status soon released them to the streets. Matthews and his friends were cautious and avoided partaking in illegal activity in front of the police.

"We would never do anything really bad," Matthews said. "We kind of had a working relationship with the cops."

After dropping out of Asbury Park High School, Matthews and Furloung participated in a large protest at the school just after the newspapers reported that American troops had invaded Cambodia. The invasion sparked protests across the country.

Matthews was camped outside of the principal's office when the head of the school came out and said: "Jesus Tom, I could never get you in this building when you were going here and now we have to get the cops to drag you out."

In Asbury Park, until the war ended, local musicians strummed and fingerpicked on their acoustic guitars and sang protest songs by artists like Arlo Guthrie. Even some Army GIs, dressed in street clothes, traveled south, along Routes 33 and 35, from their Fort Monmouth, New Jersey, headquarters to Asbury Park where they belted out protest songs in the city's folk bars. They came to Fort Monmouth from various regions where they had learned to sing and play guitar.

"People were always talking about how the hippies were spitting on the GIs coming back from Vietnam and how there was a lot of friction there, but we didn't see that," Matthews said. "The GIs hung with us."

More than 58,000 American soldiers were killed in the Vietnam War, which began in 1954 and claimed more than a million lives. During the war, communist North Vietnam and its sympathizers in the south battled the U.S.-allied South Vietnam. In 1973, President Richard Nixon ordered the withdrawal of U.S. forces and the war ended two years later when communist forces seized control of Saigon.

Some users went slightly too far and others met an untimely death due to drug overdoses in their early 20s.

"You had some drug overdoses, but they weren't as prevalent as you would think," Amato said.

Others survived bouts with drugs and alcohol, but continued to struggle with them throughout their lives. Many times, they suffered permanent damage from them.

"There are the lucky ones who have done it and stopped, but there are the other ones who had that habitual 'can't quit the shit' and they took it to extremes," Amato said. "It screws up your music. It screwed up their lives."

Drugs can be credited for destroying the lives of some members of the community. They brought other lives down unexpected paths. Some eventually became aware of the damage they were doing and quit. The potentially dire consequences forced some people to quit using drugs cold turkey. Others slowly waned themselves off of drugs. By their mid-20s and early 30s, Matthews and his friends began to realize they needed to take another route in life, instead of facing an untimely death or time in jail or a mental institution. Matthews won his second bout with speed when his interest in a Commodore 64 computer replaced his drug addiction.

Amato experimented with drugs, but never became addicted. He became involved with selling them on rare occasions. He immediately retired from this short-lived activity, when a friend told him his name was included in an investigative report on a desk in the Monmouth County Prosecutor's Office in Freehold.

"I said, 'OK, goodbye, done, I'm out of business, I'm retired, and just continued to play music," Amato said. "It's experimenting. Everybody did it."

By the late 1980s and early 1990s, pills such as Dilaudids, became the drug of choice. These prescription pain relievers can be lethal when misused. Crack and amphetamines replaced them in the 1990s.

"I'm lucky that wasn't around when I was doing stuff or we probably wouldn't be having this conversation," Matthews said.

Chapter 7
I Think I Can Get With This

"The first time I ever really liked myself was when I looked in the mirror and had a guitar in my hand." – John Luraschi, musician

John Luraschi began his musical journey as a guitar player when he was 8 after his brother, Eddie, saw a left-handed Mosrite guitar at a music store. Money was too tight in the Luraschi household to purchase a piano, which John had wished for, but Eddie had to have the guitar. The brothers decided to swap a mini-bike, which they had spent weeks building, for the guitar. John reversed the order of strings for his brother who played righty, but Eddie lost interest in playing. Cracked and dinged after one child successfully swung it at his sister, but still sounding fine, the guitar was now John's. Shortly after, John left Eddie astonished by accurately replicating guitar riffs and melodies just minutes after hearing them on the radio.

"How are you doing that?" Eddie would ask repeatedly.

"I don't know," John would respond.

John's interest grew and he started to compose short, original songs on the Mosrite.

Luraschi, who weighed less than 98 pounds until he was 23 years old, was too small for sports. Growing up, he was always the tiny and skinny kid on the Pop Warner football and Little League Baseball teams. His passion for music prevailed.

"The first time I ever really liked myself was when I looked in the mirror and had a guitar in my hand," Luraschi said. "I looked and I said, yeah, this is great, this is for me. I really like myself. I think I can get with this."

Eventually, he moved to a new neighborhood where one of the local bands needed a bassist. Bassists were a rarity in the Asbury Park area during Luraschi's youth.

"Everyone wanted to be the glory hound with the guitar," he said. "That's what you needed to get the girls."

Opportunity knocked and Luraschi switched instruments.

At the age of 12 in 1964, Luraschi joined his first band, called the Sting Rays, in Belmar. Two years later, he became the bassist of the surf band Artie Paloso and the Surftones. The latter's members spent many practices just trying to figure out how to simultaneously play and sing, he said. Luraschi spent many years in Belmar developing the rock solid bass chops music fans heard in Asbury Park.

"I sucked at first, but I could hold my own," Luraschi said. "If somebody said, 'Play in the key of G,' I knew where it was. What went on while they were playing in those keys, I couldn't really tell you."

IN CAHOOTS, IN ASBURY PARK

Though they never spoiled him with music gear, Luraschi's parents were supportive of his musical journey. They bought guitars and amplifiers when he needed them. Luraschi's mom drove him to band practices and provided her expert opinion as to whether or not each particular act was worthy of his time.

Luraschi lays the foundation with Cahoots in the late 1970s at The Stone Pony. (Photo by Lewis Bloom)

Luraschi's first bass was manufactured by Kent. After purchasing the bass, he polished and restored it, so he could trade it in for a Segovia model. The owner of the former Franks' Television shop in Asbury Park gave Luraschi the new bass and five additional dollars. Luraschi repeated the process of buying, restoring and trading for upgraded basses for more than a year.

"After a while, I got myself a good bass," he said. "It took a long time. I always wanted that Fender."

Josh Davidson

Eventually, he got it. Luraschi was self-taught on bass and never took a single lesson.

"Back then there was one book on how to play the bass," he said. "I had it and I studied and there was little information in it. So it was all touch and go."

Since gear was expensive in the era, Luraschi and his forward-thinking musical colleagues used the small microphones found in telephones as guitar pickups. They also home made their amplifiers to save money.

Luraschi persistently continued to play and eventually became a proficient, young bassist in the Asbury Park music scene, where he networked with other players and found new bands.

When he was as a young musician, a retired federal judge named Goodrich Greer was very supportive of Luraschi's development. Greer let many local musicians hone their chops using the instruments at his music store in Asbury Park. He also organized concerts where young musicians could perform. Greer's guidance was beneficial to many local musicians who came from broken homes. Luraschi's joyful childhood was followed by tragedy when he lost both parents in his early 20s. Greer encouraged Luraschi to keep practicing when he didn't feel like picking up his bass.

"He was just a goodhearted guy," Luraschi said. "He was very instrumental in keeping me in music. He saw what I couldn't see."

Luraschi didn't learn that Greer was a retired judge and war hero until he read his obituary.

Right after The Upstage closed in 1971, Luraschi and his musical colleagues ventured out to play at clubs like the Student Prince and Steve Brody's. On one night, a 19-year-old Luraschi received a call from the bassist of a band called Oz. The Jacksonville, Florida, band had traveled to play in New York and offered Luraschi what appeared to be his big break. Luraschi rehearsed with Oz and played 10 shows with them in the

IN CAHOOTS, IN ASBURY PARK

New York region. Back in Asbury Park, rumors buzzed that Luraschi had made it out of the city forever. But after two weeks, Luraschi said the band, whose members eventually became a portion of Lynyrd Skynyrd, dropped him off back in New Jersey without paying him.

"I woke up one morning with my guitar, my suitcase and that was it," he said. "They packed up and got the heck out of there. I was pissed."

It wasn't long until Luraschi found the nifty axe slinger, DeSarno, and they formed a new band in Asbury Park. Lopez, who was already playing the Hullabaloo circuit with Sonny and the Starfires, joined too.

DeSarno is known as one the Jersey Shore's best lead guitar players. The left-handed guitarist was always ahead of his game and could decipher songs that twist most musicians' brains, "Boom" Carter said.

"Nobody could touch him," he said. "I would put Ricky way before Bruce, when it comes to lead guitarists."

"He was a real nerdy looking kid," said Luraschi regarding DeSarno. "He wore penny loafers, khaki pants and a matching shirt, but he could play like Jimi Hendrix."

Other young musicians soon became jealous of the band's ability to emulate the sound of Hendrix's band. In 1974, the three musicians formed Cold, Blast & Steel, which was the first rock n' roll band to perform at the legendary Stone Pony.

Blues music played a vital role in Asbury, due in large part to the interracial mix in the area, Luraschi said. Musicians of all races enjoyed rhythm and blues music, whether it was made by Wilson Pickett, who was African-American, or The Young Rascals, a white band. During live shows, Luraschi's early bands drew laughs from the African-Americans in the audience when they attempted James Brown's music. But Luraschi's bands impressed them with their ability to play rhythm and blues, which seemed to stifle many other local bands. Occasionally, the African-

American audience members joined the bands on stage for Temptations songs, such as "My Girl."

"It was a lot of fun," Luraschi said.

Standing outside, near the front entrance of Thom McAn, Luraschi would watch an underaged future bandmate named Tony Amato being dragged by his hair out of The Upstage two floors above by his father after being caught inside. The two teenagers first met and formed a friendship at The Upstage in the late 1960s, but didn't play in a band together for about a decade.

Chapter 8
By the Strands of his Hair

"We were learning how to be us. We were learning how to play music and we were learning about life." – "Boccigalupe"

Growing up on Sunset Avenue in Asbury provided Amato with many options to occupy his time. He could take a short walk to the boardwalk or venture straight across Bond Street to The Upstage, where he spent many hours.

Margaret Potter allowed the underaged Amato to enter the club, since his father, Tony J. Amato, was the club's accountant. But sharing Joseph Carter's concerns, the senior Amato didn't want his son anywhere near the club. When the Potters were warned of an imminent arrival by Amato's father, they hid the young musician under a desk.

At 1 o'clock one morning, after discovering that his son ignored his threats about going upstairs, Amato found himself being yanked by his hair from the third floor club. The senior Amato dragged his son by the hair and pulled him down the steps.

"I don't think my feet hit any of the steps on the way down," Amato said.

That never stopped Amato from returning.

From a young age, Amato had two major interests: rock n' roll and girls. His teenage years consisted of rehearsing with bands and hanging out with his girlfriends. His musical journey began as a drummer at the age of 7. Amato took lessons at the Neptune location of Red Bank Music from a local drummer named Joe Nevolo, Sr. The lessons ended after about three weeks when Amato could no longer stand Nevolo's "pipe smoke breath." With his drum style in its early stages, Amato learned to play by emulating drum beats from his favorite records. Like many young musicians throughout Asbury Park, Amato was drawn to Sonny and The Starfires and impressed by the band's extensive repertoire. They were the first to make an impression on Amato, who also listened to a rock band led by a local guitarist named Joe Petillo, who like Sonny Kenn (front man of the Starfires) was about a half decade older than most other local musicians. Both guitarists attained local notoriety. The younger musicians were always impressed by their older counterparts in bands such as Downtown Tangiers Rocking Rhythm & Blues Band and Child. Music was a positive alternative for kids who may have otherwise been found breaking into cars, Amato said.

One day, Amato went with his mother to a Dave Clark Five show at Convention Hall. The pair received a free entrance into the venue since a close family friend, Henry Vaccaro, Sr., was an Asbury Park city councilman.

Eventually, Amato joined his first band called Ecstasy. The band was also the first for a red-headed, 14-year-old lead singer named Patti Scialfa, Springsteen's current wife and bandmate. The band's lineup also included Jerry Armstrong on guitar and Brian Sayer on bass. The 13-year-old

IN CAHOOTS, IN ASBURY PARK

Amato always remained persistent in spite of the challenges presented by a scene dominated by musicians over the age of 18. Rather than finding a ride to practice, Amato carried his drums to rehearsals.

Matthews had an extremely short stint with the band. Living on Bond Street and attending Holy Spirit High School in Asbury Park, Matthews appeared at Ecstasy's rehearsal pad in attempt to replace the band's recently departed bassist. He jammed the three-chord song "Gloria" for about two hours, before the band caught on that he didn't know any others.

"Two hours of Gloria is enough," Amato told him at the time. Playing with the windows open, the tryout made about 60 neighbors complain to the police about noise in the vicinity of the lake. After a short-lived (four hour) music career following a tryout with Ecstasy in 1967, Matthews retired to life as a fan.
Matthews' love of music drove him to stay involved in the music scene.

His stocky build equipped him to carry Ecstasy's amps, before he watched them practice in the kitchen of Asbury Park's Windsor Hotel. Matthews was part of a group of about 30 non-musicians who were integral components of the Asbury Park music scene's key bands, Amato said.

"Whether (Tom) was on stage or not, he was still part of the band," Amato said. "It was one big, happy family back then."

The group of fans would follow the band to local shows, including those at Ecstasy member Patti Scialfa's house in Asbury Park's northern neighbor, Deal, a beach club in nearby Loch Arbor or in someone's basement. The group of fans didn't flock to a particular band; they enjoyed the entire mix of bands in the area. News of local shows or parties with live music spread mostly through word of mouth, as flyers, cell phones or computers were nonexistent, Matthews said.

Josh Davidson

"One guy would say something to another guy, it would spread and then later on you would show up and say, what the hell is this?" Matthews said. "Back then, we just liked hearing music."

In the 1960s, teenaged Asbury Park musicians learned from one another instead of trying to show up their counterparts. Jealously among separate bands was rare, as musicians focused on improving their chops, Amato said. Asbury Park was the central location for early teenagers from areas throughout the county to meet and form bands. They came from Monmouth and Ocean counties and made their way to basements throughout Asbury. Most line ups lacked a few pieces when bands first formed. Band members would complete their line ups by networking and meeting other musicians. Some kids didn't have experience in the instrument they brought with them to a local basement, but they learned as they went along.

"All of the sudden, musicians were meeting each other," Amato said. "Asbury was a melting pot. That's how bands got started."

Outsiders tried to break in to the inner circle of musicians, but only the true survived.

"We were learning how to be us," Amato said. "We were learning how to play music and we were learning about life."

Asbury Park's musicians didn't have aspirations of fame or fortune, at that age, they simply played music. Young men and women in the city had three choices: music, school or Vietnam, Amato said.

"Some of us chose music and some didn't have a choice and ended up in Vietnam," he said.

Amato's first-ever performance was before a dense summer weekend beach crowd at the Deal Casino. Lenient drinking and driving laws left the clubs packed with people excited to experience Asbury Park's sights and sounds. Built-in crowds eased the burden of bands who didn't have to worry about drawing people to their shows. Early on, Amato was influenced by The Dave Clark Five, Elvis Presley and The Beatles. Amato knew he would remain a musician from the first note he played.

"It's just something that you want to do," he said. "It's not like God decided that I am going to be musician, but it's just something that is inside of you."

When he was 13, a cover band that included Amato landed a gig opening for the Young Rascals at Convention Hall. Early on Amato got slightly nervous at performances, but consistently playing before large crowds with many stellar musicians made him better at his craft.

Amato continued to play the drums, but started to tool around on an organ downstairs in Vaccaro's office building. A return visit to Convention Hall for a performance by The Rascals sparked a change in the 17-year-old's primary instruments. Amato quickly became enamored by the keyboard stylings of The Rascals' Felix Cavaliere and the sounds the instrument could produce. He was also floored by the playing of the master of the Hammond B-3 organ, Jimmy Smith.

"When I started playing keyboards I was jumping back and forth between keyboards, drums and bass guitar," he said. "Then, finally, The Young Rascals made that decision. When The Young Rascals came out, I heard the B-3 with Felix Cavaliere and was like, yeah!"

Amato spent hours developing his own personal style of playing.

"It took me a while to learn how to play it, but I picked it up," Amato said.

Amato played the straight-ahead rock n' roll and rhythm and blues of Sam & Dave and Sam Cooke before delving into heavy organ rock by Deep Purple. He later experimented with synthesizer-based music from Emerson, Lake & Palmer and then the jazz/fusion music of Chick Corea.

"I got into different styles of music: jazz/fusion, rock, blues, R&B, soul. Then I put it together," Amato said.

Amato continued performing at venues like the Knights of Columbus Hall in Philadelphia while he attended military school at the Admiral Farragut Academy in Pine Beach, New Jersey. Due to his age, some clubs still remained off limits and he gigged more consistently when he reached the legal drinking age.

Amato builds melodies on the organ with Cahoots in 1977 at The Stone Pony. (Photo by Lewis Bloom)

IN CAHOOTS, IN ASBURY PARK

He first played a Lowrey organ through a Plush guitar amp before being introduced to the Farfisa organ, which was manufactured in Italy. For many players, the latter instrument was the alternative to the B-3. The Farfisa looked like a briefcase, was carried with one hand and included similar features to the B-3, including its rolling tone generator that gave the organ its distinct sound. The keyboard could produce adequate sounds on its own, but ultimately couldn't compare to the B-3, Amato said.

"It just doesn't come that close," he said. "There is nothing like playing a B-3. For one, it's the sound. Also, there is really certain kind of feel and touch when you play the organ. It's not just the sound; it's the feel you get, when you play the keys."

Even today, keyboards and synthesizers are built to emulate the B-3 sound. The B-3's growl just can't be reproduced by any of its kind, Amato said.

"There is no replacing the sound of a B-3," he said.
The B-3 is not used as much today, as the modern version doesn't compare to the 1958 model. Due to technological advancements, Hammond discontinued the rolling tone generator inside its organs.

"They were trying to fix something that was never broken," Amato said.

As a result, Amato stopped using the B-3 for a long time period. He now owns two.

Amato continued to experiment and perform on the keyboards, which were gaining prominence both in Asbury Park and mainstream music. Amato's first band as a keyboard player, Nicky Don and Company, allowed him to branch out to bars other than the Wonder Bar. The band steadily played top 40 music and songs such as "My Way" by Frank Sinatra at bars like the Gold Digger in Asbury Park. The band's front man and bassist, Nicky Donofrio, built most of its set list, but the song choices would grow via improvisation and audience requests. Still only 18, Amato's band mates' ages ranged from the late 20s to early 40s. As a result of playing with more experienced musicians, Amato became less nervous when performing. Donofrio turned out to be an exceptional teacher and mentor to Amato, as he started to perform more frequently.

Amato eventually left the band in 1972 and performed with Brothers and Sisters for the next year and a half. The band also included Nick Saviro, Karen Manetta and Margo and Ronny Harrison.

He started primarily running the band's sound system and eventually played some shows as the band's keyboardist.

It was all a learning process," Amato said. "Everything was building up and building up. I was learning another thing — how to mix a band and make a band sound good."

He also continued to experiment sonically with the keyboards. He learned how to manipulate the Hammond B-3 organ's internal reverb effects and how to externally modify the instrument so he could add effects like a wah-wah pedal or additional reverbs. Modifying the instrument came easy after Amato gained more experience running sound, but he still preferred to keep his B-3 pure.

"It was just another learning process," Amato said. "I really wasn't playing (live) much until maybe 1974 when things really changed around."

Chapter 9
Schrebs

"We were part of a musical family." - Steve "Schrebs" Schraeger

Some might describe one initial meeting of Steve "Schrebs" Schraeger and Tony "Boccigalupe" Amato as uncanny. However, when you consider the factors such as "1974," "Asbury Park" and "rock n' roll," you get a typical rock band story.

The story begins when Amato, who was in Brothers and Sisters at the time, stopped at The Warehouse, on Asbury Park's 4th Avenue, to watch Schraeger's band Dayz perform.

Amato, who lived across the street, began enjoying some cocktails with Schraeger, who was already drunk. Eventually, Amato noticed a drunken Schraeger was seconds away from getting his ass kicked by a group of drunk, off-duty state troopers who were looking for him. He grabbed Schraeger and pulled him out of the club, which eventually became the Fast Lane.

"Get in the car, let's go," Amato demanded.

The two men have been close friends ever since.

"Somebody tried to beat me up, but he saved me," Schraeger said. "Right away, the guy became my best friend. He saved me from being beat up. I was very impressed."

They also forged the beginning of a musical partnership, which became a piece of Asbury Park's history.

Schraeger meets his idol, jazz drummer Gene Krupa, as a child. Schraeger's cousin, Sharon Knudson, and her boyfriend at the time, George Evens, stand behind them. (Photo courtesy of Schraeger)

"I have a lot of respect for Tony," Schraeger said. "He is very knowledgeable and a very smart guy."

Dayz formed in 1973, when Luraschi and Schraeger decided to start a new band, after their preceding group, Cold, Blast and Steel, had disbanded. The band also included Mike Scialfa on Fender Rhodes keyboard and a very young Stan Jankowski (who later became known as Stan Steele) on guitar, before adding Tommy LaBella on saxophone. Jankowski and Luraschi had jammed frequently at Luraschi's house

IN CAHOOTS, IN ASBURY PARK

before the band formed. The band covered many musical styles ranging from Billy Cobham, a jazz drummer who played with Miles Davis and Mahavishnu Orchestra, to The Beatles. Rock was the predominant style of choice for the band, which frequently played at The Warehouse and other Asbury Park venues, such as The Stone Pony. The band ventured north to perform in Jamesburg, New Jersey, but mostly stayed local. The band hosted jam nights at The Warehouse and spent a lot of time rehearsing, before disbanding after one year.

Schraeger began playing drums on his self-made kit at age 12. His interest grew when his cousin took him to see the jazz drummer Gene Krupa, who played with Benny Goodman in the mid-1930s. Schraeger's parents bought him a drum set after the vibrant big band drummer told him to get one and practice his favorite songs.

"Then The Beatles came out and I said, I've got to do that," Schraeger said.

He experimented with fusion as he grew up, but straightforward "4-4" rock n' roll was always his style of choice. Schraeger's simplistic playing technique gave him an edge when locking in with his rhythm section counterparts.

"If you play straight ahead, locking in with the bass player will come naturally," Schraeger said. "If you never try to overplay and just keep it straight, a good bass player will lock right into it."

Solid chemistry also allows bands to evolve, improve and experience magical moments during jam sessions, he said. In 1973, the 23-year-old Schraeger felt that chemistry with Luraschi and joined Cold, Blast and Steel, where he complemented Lopez in a two-drum configuration which included DeSarno on lead guitar. Lopez was the last member to join the band, after being fired from The E Street Band, Schraeger said.

"If one of us was playing low on the high hat, the other drummer would play up, so we complemented each other," Schraeger said.

Schraeger drives a steady beat with Cahoots in the late 1970s at The Stone Pony. (Photo by Lewis Bloom)

Schraeger's first professional band played straight ahead rock n' roll originals and covers from artists like ZZ Top. Music was a profession for the band, which spent its typical days practicing, writing songs and playing shows mainly around the Jersey Shore.

"We were busy," Schraeger said. "We were children. We were just learning every day. We were learning what the music business was all about."

Cold, Blast and Steel disbanded after about a year and a half.

Many musicians knew that flourishing in the solid music scene could result in a full-time, professional music career. When playing packed Asbury Park clubs, musicians would quickly learn if they had what it takes.

IN CAHOOTS, IN ASBURY PARK

"You could get in front of a packed house and if you could control (the crowd) and get your music across – that was your ticket," Schraeger said. "It told you then and there that you could play music and get better at it. If you failed, then you had work to do."

The crowd's reaction would many times determine the length of a band's music career.

"If you could win over the audience, you could play anywhere," Schraeger said. "It didn't matter how big the room was. Confidence was a big thing. You had to know you could go out there and take them deep."

It was an era when musicians like Schraeger formed lifelong bonds with their "brothers."

"It was very much a happening scene, similar to Liverpool," he said. "There were a lot of good musicians, who knew each other. It was like a brotherhood. We were part of a musical family."

Chapter 10
The Audition

"Bob Seger's line in 'Rock and Roll Never Forgets' is: 'Well all Chuck's children are out there playing his licks.' We were all Chuck's children." – John Oeser, musician

It was 1969 when John Oeser sang from the back of a fast food chicken restaurant, next to a large, loud pressure cooker, and became introduced to life as a performer. His sweet, booming vocal style did not only catch the attention of his co-workers, who were surprised of their comrade's talent. Only singing to pass the time as he worked and not realizing he was auditioning, Oeser soon was introduced to one of his first band members, standing out front.

"You didn't think anybody was going to hear you out front," Oeser said. "Somebody heard me out front and he asked to talk to me."

IN CAHOOTS, IN ASBURY PARK

Before this "audition," the teenager had never thought of being a professional musician, as he sang along to the sounds of the Beach Boys and Motown at his home in Toms River. Playing sports took up most of his time, though he did pick up a guitar and learned a few chords after seeing The Beatles on "The Ed Sullivan Show." Oeser eventually met other guitarists at school. As his interest in music increased, he sought their help in learning basic aspects of the instrument, such as chord positions.

Oeser still took the offer to join his first band and was soon learning The Allman Brothers Band's songs with them in a very modest rehearsal space.

"We piled into this guy's bedroom — in a split level that was probably about 8' by 10,'" he said.

The band had all of the key components of a late 1960s band: an organist, a bass guitarist playing through a double cabinet amplifier, an electric guitarist who played a Marshall stack and a drummer. The huge amps, five band members, full drum kit and Shure public address system were packed into a tiny room, playing songs that are now categorized as classic rock.

When he wasn't practicing with his band, Oeser listened to many styles of music, and learned a lot along the way. He struggled to obtain a clear, terrestrial radio signal in his hometown and was only able to access a few radio stations.

"WNEW (a Maryland radio station) hadn't even started yet," Oeser said. "MMR out of Philadelphia only came on at eight or nine o'clock at night."

Before switching to a full music format, WMMR shared the airwaves with a sports station that broadcasted during the day.

"There was a jazz station out of North Jersey where once in a while you could hear some R&B and soul music, as well as jazz," he said. "But that always wasn't a good catch."

Even long before Oeser's spontaneous "audition" in the back of a chicken restaurant, he practiced singing along to records at home. With only a handful of local bands to keep his interest, Oeser learned from the radio. Oeser's avid interest in music expanded when the songs of four young, mop-topped British men hit the U.S. airwaves.

"When The Beatles came out it was like, oh my god, what the heck is this?" Oeser said. "You heard that on the radio and it was so different — the harmonies of the Everly Brothers and the drive of Chuck Berry, which was a pretty cool mixture."

The Beatles brought a look and style to the U.S. that teenagers weren't accustomed to, Oeser said. As records sales surged, music stores sold more instruments. Boys strung together open guitar chords with the hopes of learning a full song and impressing the opposite sex. Early in junior high school, Oeser tooled around with a guitar, but not the idea of joining a band.

"You would hear The Beatles, you would beg your parents for a guitar and you would bang on that for a while," he said.

The little transistor radio Oeser's parents bought for him, became his early music teacher. Oeser now found himself tuning into popular radio stations, like WABC and WMCA, and singing along to Beach Boys' songs. Oeser also learned to sing the hits of Stevie Wonder, Smokey Robinson and many female singers, and began to use his record player to train with more precision.

"You would put your finger on the record player to slow it down a little, so you could try and understand what the hell Mick Jagger was saying," he said.

IN CAHOOTS, IN ASBURY PARK

Thanks to cable, satellite radio and the Internet, today's music fans can enjoy hundreds of radio stations clearly. Years before the introduction of file sharing, excited fans like Oeser would physically deliver records like James Cotton's "Rocket 88" to one another, sharing their amazement upon discovering the musical proficiency that the Mississippi bluesman demonstrated in his pulsating harmonica interludes.

Rhythmically, Oeser's young voice emulated that of Levi Stubbs of The Four Tops and Otis Redding. The loud singing volume of females like Fontella Bass and Aretha Franklin also shaped Oeser's singing style.

"Female singers had a huge influence on me," said Oeser, who never experienced gospel on Sunday mornings. "Not that I could ever sing like them. There was a, while very free, very what I found out to be church-based style that they had. They didn't sing the way that Lutherans sang at church."

Oeser continued playing with his first band while learning as much as possible about his craft. The band played the music of bands like The Doors, which was considered standard band material at the time. Though there weren't many local singers or bands to learn from in Toms River, Oeser occasionally watched his older friends practice. Just out of high school, his friends later became successful in the famous New York Rock n' Roll Ensemble. On nights off, he and his friends would visit The Upstage. Word of mouth had made Upstage the "school of rock" for up and coming musicians, and opened Oeser's eyes and ears to unscripted, improvised performances. The Upstage became the institution where Oeser was schooled on rock n' roll.

At The Upstage, Oeser was astonished as he closely watched musicians who had never played together before, call out a key and completely reinvent songs from the radio. Oeser, whose band tended to stick with original song arrangements, watched many future legends transform "Twist and Shout" into something much more eclectic than its album version.

Oeser would sneak past his parents at home on his way to The Upstage with his band mates late on a Friday or Saturday night when the music began, only to sneak back in the house at 2 or 3 a.m. Despite his parent's warnings not to go to The Upstage during the school year, Oeser would leave the house once they went to bed, drive to Asbury Park and deal with the consequences when he returned home.

Though he never played at The Upstage, Oeser still absorbed every moment and learned musicianship from players who would become some of the greatest in the country. The club's distinct sights and sounds influenced Oeser along his own musical journey.

"It was a whole different influence," Oeser said. "There wasn't a place like that in the Toms River area, where you could go and hear music or work and jam with other musicians."

Though only separated geographically by 25 miles across the Garden State Parkway, Toms River and Asbury Park existed on separate cultural stratospheres. The Upstage became a center of the New Jersey hippie movement where teenagers wore their hair long and didn't trust people over 30. Oeser watched characters like Lopez and "Big Bobby" Williams create mayhem on the club's stage. The wild expression pasted permanently in Lopez's eyes earned him the lifelong nickname "Mad Dog." Oeser watched both drummers' loud and crazy antics from the audience, but still hadn't become their colleague.

"From my point of view, I was a visitor to The Upstage," he said.

It wasn't long before Oeser and his Toms River friends experienced the buzz circulating around Asbury Park about a guy named Springsteen. Even before he became a rock star, fans would travel from surrounding counties waiting for Springsteen to show up at an Asbury Park club.

IN CAHOOTS, IN ASBURY PARK

"He became the star of the show," Oeser said.

Oeser and his bandmates ventured around the Jersey Shore, playing gigs and experiencing the music that lined the Ocean Avenue strip that stretched across Monmouth and Ocean counties. Since they were below the drinking age of 21, they would obtain a state permit so they could perform in bars. The band played Seaside Heights, New Jersey, which had become a resort town, filled with patrons interested in singing and dancing to familiar music.

"It was a nice little music scene down (at the Jersey Shore), especially since you had the boardwalk and a lot of clubs in Seaside, so we managed to be able to pick up gigs there," he said.

The Big Band music enjoyed by older people, like Oeser's parents, was predominant in Seaside Heights, but Good Time Charlie's, on the Boulevard, hired straight rock n' roll bands.

"That was one of the true rock n' roll venues in Seaside Heights where you would just go and play and not worry about having matching outfits on or a set list," Oeser said.

The bar's owner, Jimmy O'Donnell, saw a niche in catering to the rock n' roll crowds who visited the Jersey Shore.

"He liked rock n' roll music and that was all he hired," Oeser said.

Oeser grabs the audience's attention with some R&B influenced vocals in the late 1970s at The Stone Pony. (Photo by Lewis Bloom)

Oeser played both empty and packed venues on the Jersey Shore, while continuing to learn songs on his record player. His band played songs by Chuck Berry and other artists whose music kept the bars packed with people who would repeatedly order drinks. Attending Toms River

IN CAHOOTS, IN ASBURY PARK

High School, Oeser also played battle of the bands events in local high school gymnasiums.

When he wasn't sneaking into The Upstage, Oeser would dodge his parents and find his way into Asbury Park's Student Prince or Gold Diggers clubs. Only authorized as a player but not a patron of bars, it was a rare occasion when Oeser could sneak in to watch a show. He eventually snuck his way into the Student Prince to see The Sundance Blues Band. There, he found a new "school," closely watching Springsteen perform with the band, which transformed Carole King's "Smackwater Jack" into a signature dish.

"It was just a great atmosphere," Oeser said. "(Springsteen) would play what he liked to play, whether it was something that you knew or not. The concept that I learned there was that whatever the song is, just do it well. Just do it heartfelt. Go out and give it every bit. Make it like it's the last song that you're ever going to sing. That was pretty enlightening."

With its oversized garage doors, the Wonder Bar was another venue worthy of avoiding his parents' ire. There, "Stormin'" Norman Seldin & the Joyful Noyze had a drummer who played standing up and Clemons on the saxophone.

"I was too young to get into the place, but you could stand outside and hear all of the music that you wanted to," Oeser said.

As Oeser grew older, money was a necessity for maintaining his music career, but he still played for the sheer joy of baring his soul to an audience. Other disciples of The Beatles and Rolling Stones developed careers through the opportunities so many Asbury Park clubs offered to young musicians. They borrowed riffs and rhythms of 1960s radio, as they developed styles of their own.

Josh Davidson

"Bob Seger's line in 'Rock and Roll Never Forgets' is: 'Well all Chuck's children are out there playing his licks,'" Oeser said. "We were all Chuck's children."

In the early 1970s, Oeser's career progressed as he hopped along the East Coast, bouncing through separate bands along the way. The singer left his first band and began touring as a performer with a few other acts. To his own dismay, he began playing in doo wop "show bands," which were much more structured than the bands he saw in Asbury Park. The show bands played commercial music, wore matching outfits and followed choreographed moves. Though educational, the experience wasn't enjoyable, lacking the raw approach and musical complexity he had carefully studied in Asbury.

"It just went against my grain completely," he said. "The musicianship wasn't front and center. The people wanted a show."

The band's musicians were solid and many of the singers are still playing the circuit today, but the product was very structured and simple. Eventually, Oeser landed in the Pompano Beach area of Florida with one of the show bands, which he eventually left, before heading back to Asbury Park.

Oeser made his way back to New Jersey in 1975 and stumbled upon a newspaper ad placed by a rhythm guitarist and singer named George Theiss and his band Doo-Da, which had already been together for a few years. Theiss, who had previously played in Rusty Chain, after being in a Freehold Borough-based band called The Castiles, transformed the Doo-Da's s jam band style into a straight-ahead rock n' roll sound. Oeser landed the gig, playing R&B, early Springsteen, The Eagles, Elton John and non-commercial club music at local clubs such as the Osprey in Manasquan. Doo-Da played many other clubs and the college circuit at colleges in New York and Pennsylvania and Princeton and Rutgers universities in New Jersey.

IN CAHOOTS, IN ASBURY PARK

The band had the largest personnel of any Oeser band to that date including a lead vocalist, guitarist, saxophonist, keyboardist, bassist and drummer. The short-lived band broke up following a major show backing up The Platters in Pennsylvania.

Chapter 11
Sidewalks

"As we grew older, things started changing and then Bruce started singing more. Towards the end, we were just butting heads, because he wanted to do one thing and I wanted to do something else. It just fell apart." – George Theiss, musician

Growing up in the country, surrounded by farmland, the 12-year-old George Theiss had minimal exposure to the mania other pre-teens were experiencing via the mainstream rock n' roll and doo wop music which began sweeping the nation in the 1950s.

The radio airwaves that surrounded his Freehold household were dominated by the likes of Pat Boone, Little Richard, Connie Stevens, Connie Francis and old-time country music. Elvis Presley, who had

IN CAHOOTS, IN ASBURY PARK

already become a heartthrob for teen girls and an idol for young men, did not grab Theiss' attention. While visiting a friend at a farm across the street from his parent's home, he began to notice an acoustic guitar sitting in the corner. He tooled around with the instrument repeatedly and his interest increased. By Christmas, Theiss had his own Roy Rogers plastic guitar. As soon as he witnessed The Beatles invade the U.S. with a new brand of mania in 1964, Theiss became a serious guitar player. He continued listening to musicians like The Rolling Stones, Clapton, Hendrix and Jimmy Page.

"I used to sleep with my guitar," said Theiss, who was born in Newark, New Jersey, and moved to Freehold when he was 6. "I would go to bed, lay down and just lay there playing it. I was listening to records and trying to copy them – that kind of thing. I think a lot of guys did that and still do. I wanted to be a rock n' roll star, I still do, but you know then reality sets in and eventually it does."

Impressing the opposite sex also incentivized Theiss to play music. Though his uncle owned a violin factory, Theiss' parents weren't heavily into music. His father at one point played for the Newark Bears minor league baseball team. Still in the infant stages of his musical development, Theiss was 13 when he joined his first band, The Five Diamonds.

"I couldn't even play anything, really, in The Five Diamonds," Theiss said. "Things just started developing. Out of that whole group of people, I think we had one guy that knew how to play guitar."

The short, round Italian kid, named Mike DeLuise, could play all of the typical guitar riffs and chords on his red, sparkly Gretsch guitar.

Though the band didn't make it too far out of its rehearsal space, the experience gave its members their first exposure to being part of a group. The band eventually evolved into The Sierras, which included Theiss on rhythm guitar and vocals, Bart Haynes on drums and vocals, DeLuise on guitar and Vinnie Roslin on bass.

Josh Davidson

In 1965, as The Sierras attempted to turn noise into music in Haynes' half of a two-family house on Freehold's Center Street, a gruff-mannered Army Veteran named Gordon "Tex" Vinyard entered their lives. Vinyard, a factor worker in his late 30s who lived in the second half of the house, not-so-politely requested that they "lower the noise." A few days later, Theiss, the band's lead singer and rhythm guitarist, visited the Vinyard residence to apologize for the "racket." Interested in working with The Sierras, Vinyard asked Theiss to bring the band to his half of the house. Vinyard's living room became the band's rehearsal hall and things rapidly became more serious. The Sierras changed its named to The Castiles and added multi-instrumentalist Paul Popkin and Frank Marziotti on bass. The 24-year-old Marziotti was nine years older than his bandmates.

"He was a great guy who played with us for a little while," Theiss said.

Marziotti was replaced by Curt Fluhr by mid-1966, just before Haynes left the band to join the Marine Corps. He was replaced on drums by Vinny Maniello. Haynes deployed to Vietnam a year after leaving the band. On Oct. 22, 1967, the 19-year-old lance corporal was killed by mortar fire in the Quang Tri province of Vietnam. He was the first soldier from Freehold to die in the Vietnam War.

In 1966, Theiss was dating a Freehold Regional High School freshman named Ginny Springsteen, whose brother, Bruce, played guitar. In search of a new lead guitarist, Theiss knocked on the door of the now former Springsteen residence on South Street in Freehold Borough. Springsteen, who had just left his first band, The Rogues, followed Theiss to Vinyard's house and became the lead guitarist/vocalist of The Castiles.

The band continued to practice as Tex's wife, Marion, kept them hydrated with sodas from the local supermarket and filled their bellies with sandwiches. In August 1965, the band ventured out of the Vinyards' living room to play its first gig at a pizzeria. They moved on to the

IN CAHOOTS, IN ASBURY PARK

auditorium St. Rose of Lima School in Freehold, followed by gigs at swim clubs, supermarkets and Veterans of Foreign Wars halls, and roller rinks in Freehold and nearby Matawan. The band had repeat performances at the Surf 'N' See Club in Sea Bright and Freehold Regional High School, where The Castiles played at its own junior prom.

Luraschi was impressed when he first saw The Castiles perform at a high school dance. The band's members were proficient at spinning their favorite songs in their own creative direction, he said.

"All of the girls were going for George and not Bruce," Luraschi said.

In November 1966, The Castiles made its first trip to Greenwich Village for a gig at the legendary Café Wha? In January 1961, Bob Dylan took a subway to Café Wha? at 115 MacDougal St., and played a short set of Woody Guthrie songs to an audience at half capacity, just after arriving in New York City for the first time. Frequented by poet Allen Ginsberg and eventually Hendrix, who was discovered there by manager Chas Chandler, the venue's stage was the first stop in the careers of many bands, musicians and comedians like Peter, Paul & Mary and Richard Pryor.

Maniello transported his drums in his own car and Vinyard drove the rest of the band members and equipment to gigs.

"Vinny didn't really like taking any other equipment, except his drums," Theiss said. "We would pretty much load everything into Tex's car."

This included the 8-foot-tall PA speakers Vinyard built with a friend.

"They had two of those and he would stick those in the trunk," Theiss said. "They would be sticking out of the trunk, with our amps, guitars and everything else. I don't know how he did it."

Each time the band headed north on the New Jersey Turnpike for one of many gigs at Café Wha?, Vinyard was pulled over by a police officer.

109

Theiss routinely directed a wise-crack at the cop, and Vinyard just as certainly received a ticket.

As soon as he pulled the car over, "The first thing Tex would say was, 'Theiss, keep your mouth shut,'" Theiss recalled.

By the time he reached high school, Theiss was playing and looking the part of a rock n' roller. One day, Theiss, Springsteen and Popkin decided to change their look.

"One day we all just went into the bathroom and combed our hair down," Theiss said. "It wasn't any longer. We just combed it down, so it looked like the Beatles."

Eventually, after being told his hair was too long, Theiss tried emulating the late 1950s, "Brylcreem" style by combing his hair back with a curl hanging down the front. The Castiles' dress didn't resemble The Beatles until they played at Café Wha?, where they donned military jackets and tall boots, resembling the cover of The Beatles' "Sgt. Pepper's Lonely Hearts Club Band" album. The Castiles mostly played covers of songs by The Rolling Stones, The Beatles, The Who, Cream, Hendrix and John Mayall. To this day, Theiss is enamored by the audiences' overly enthusiastic reaction to a cover called "Sidewalks."

"There were just two chords in the whole song, just A and G," Theiss said. "It had almost a skip-beat kind of a thing to it and people loved that song. To this day, I can't figure out why."

Theiss made up different lyrics each time the band played the song and frequently heard fans scream the song's name during concerts. "That song became our 'Free Bird,'" he said.

As they reached the mid-point of many songs, The Castiles broke out into free-style, psychedelic jam sessions.

In May 1966 the band recorded for the first time at a studio in Brick Township, New Jersey. They started with "That's What You Get" and

IN CAHOOTS, IN ASBURY PARK

"Baby I," two songs penned by Springsteen and Theiss during the drive to the studio.

In late 1967, Vinyard and a friend opened a club in Freehold called The Left Foot, which bared a close resemblance to Café Wha? and many of the hip Greenwich Village venues. The Castiles performed at the grand opening of the venue located at 37 Throckmorton Street, across from the bus station. Vinyard kept a tight rein to prevent any incidents at the venue, which remained open for more than a year.

"That was a cool place to be," Theiss said. "Kids could just come out and play music."

After well more than 100 live performances, a creative clash between Springsteen and Theiss led to the disbandment of The Castiles in August 1968.

"As we grew older, things started changing and then Bruce started singing more," Theiss said. "Towards the end, we were just butting heads, because he wanted to do one thing and I wanted to do something else. It just fell apart.

"We both were developing this bull-headed, I'm the leader of the band thing," Theiss said. "And finally that was it."

Springsteen, who began hanging out with Van Zandt on a more frequent basis, formed the band Earth in 1968.

Springsteen and Theiss returned to the old Freehold Borough neighborhood in May 2002 for a dedication of Vinyard Park, located across from Jackson and Center streets. Springsteen, who during the ceremony jokingly described Vinyard, as a "terribly grumpy, old bastard," recalled when Vinyard returned home from work on Fridays with his paycheck before heading to the local music store to purchase microphones, guitar strings and other essential equipment for The Castiles.

"Tex was somebody who opened his house completely, opened his heart completely and opened his wallet to us," said Springsteen, during the ceremony. "(He) allowed us to come in and turn it up as loud as we wanted, when all of the other adults were trying to get us to turn it down."

Springsteen described the Vinyards and the other adults across the country who supported local bands as "the unsung heroes of rock n' roll who, without which, we wouldn't have had a place to practice and hone our craft."

"I couldn't quantify how much it meant to my musical development and just to my life, in general," Springsteen said. "As you go on, you carry with you a big part of the texture of the town from which you came from. I've carried that with me long since I've moved out of Freehold."

Years after he left The Castiles, Springsteen needed someone to co-sign a loan he required to purchase new musical equipment. Vinyard, who no longer managed Springsteen, signed above the line.

Vinyard was 32 when he first met the 15-year-old Theiss.

"My mother wasn't crazy about Tex, but Tex was always there," Theiss said. "He kept us in line."

Many years later, Theiss had an audition with Warner Bros. Records. Hoping Vinyard would go with him, Theiss struck up a conversation with his former manager. But Vinyard began saying things that made Theiss hesitant about exposing him to the label's staff.

"So I went and did the audition without him," Theiss said. "At that point, I was like I'm an adult; I'm not a kid anymore. But he kind of felt like I stabbed him in the back. He was really pissed off at me and didn't talk to me for about a year."

Now an adult, Theiss struggled to explain to Vinyard that he was no longer a child without hurting his former manager's feelings. The two men ran into each other and began speaking again for about a year shortly before Vinyard died in 1989.

Being manager of The Castiles was Vinyard's first involvement in the music industry, Theiss said. When Vinyard began the role, he had been laid off from his job and was home, collecting unemployment, Theiss said.

"He was a big personality," Theiss said.

After the Castiles disbanded, Theiss joined Rusty Cain at the age of 18. Theiss gave Rusty Chain's soft sound a harder edge, before he left and joined Doo-Da. Theiss died of lung cancer in July 2018.

Chapter 12
In Cahoots

"The band wasn't really together all that long before Tony became a part of it. He kind of showed up and we never could get rid of him again." - Oeser

Doo-Da had reached a crossroads when it received the opportunity to go on tour to back up The Platters, one of the most successful vocal groups of the 1950s. While some of the band members balked at the offer, Theiss, Oeser and the band's bassist joined The Platters for about three weeks.

When the band's agent came up short on the promised pay, Theiss and the rest of the band quit.

"When it came time to get paid, they handed us money and we looked at it and went, 'Where's the rest?'" Theiss said.

The next day Theiss and Oeser headed to Asbury Park and inquired about new band opportunities. Searching for a new project, Theiss and

IN CAHOOTS, IN ASBURY PARK

Oeser strolled into a small club and found a band called Dayz. Oeser observed what he called a "very, very obnoxious lead singer" fronting the band.

"He announced for the first time to everybody that this is our last gig," Oeser said.

Viewing the astonished look on the rest of the band's faces, but knowing the lineup was established, Oeser and Theiss decided to strike up a conversation with the members. During the encounter, Mike Scialfa didn't say a word, but Schraeger's personality and short-breathed, raspy Jewish accent stood out from the beginning.

"To hear Schraeger's voice for the very first time definitely takes you aback," Oeser said. "You knew he was a character."

This was one of the conversations which led to the formation of Cahoots. Luraschi made the first move towards putting together Cahoots' first practice session at the Elberon, New Jersey, home he shared with his wife.

"Bring your stuff down," Luraschi told his future bandmates. "We'll rehearse in my basement and let's see what we can do."

Oeser was instantly impressed by the band's musicianship.

"They were indeed characters, Schraeger especially. He still is. And then when we met Tony. Here we go, another character — crazy little bastard," Oeser said.

After playing a few songs together, the band smelled success. Theiss and Oeser immediately noticed that Cahoots had a tight rhythm section of Schraeger and Luraschi. The area lacked fundamentally solid bass players who could lock in with a drummer.

"You had too many bass players that were frustrated lead guitar players," Oeser said. "All of the sudden we had this rhythm section that was really tight and sounded as good as any recording we had ever heard, so we were really impressed.

"John was always on Steve's ass, pumping him up to move faster or slow it down, but they worked great together," Theiss said

Many times, Luraschi would start drinking Jack Daniels whiskey shortly before breaking into an argument with Schraeger. The two fought on many occasions, and one night Luraschi did donuts with his car in the parking lot near The Stone Pony as he tried to chase down Schraeger, Theiss said.

Theiss had already practiced diligently to develop a steady rhythm hand on guitar when he was younger. Roslin's brother, who played in a country and western band, first showed the teenaged Theiss how to play with an open tuning on the guitar. Theiss developed a style of tuning his guitar to open E and using only one finger on the neck to play barre chords. The technique restricted Theiss solely to major chords, but took the focus off of his left hand and allowed him to develop a very solid rhythm hand. During a gig in Shrewsbury, New Jersey, Theiss tuned his guitar to standard tuning and stuck with it as his predominant tuning for the remainder of his career. Later, when he played rhythm guitar in Cahoots, he was able to closely synchronize his right hand with Schraeger's snare drum and high hat hits.

Oeser was also enamored by LaBella, whose jazzy notes scampered above the music.

"It was like having a super lead guitar player in your band," said Oeser when describing LaBella's playing style. "He had a higher tone that really cut right through. It really added a very interesting aspect to the sound of our band."

Strong vocal harmonies and dual keyboards filled out Cahoots' sound.

"Tommy LaBella was just wailing over the top of it," Oeser said. "It was a very cool sound."

IN CAHOOTS, IN ASBURY PARK

At one point, LaBella contemplated leaving the band to focus on furthering his education, but Theiss said he convinced the saxophonist to stick with his music.

Shortly after Cahoots' inception, Oeser noticed Amato showing up at rehearsals. As he started to transition out of Brothers and Sisters, Amato was already hanging out with his future Cahoots band mates at The Warehouse, as the merger of Dayz and Doo-Dah progressed.

Amato prepares for a performance with Cahoots in 1977 at The Stone Pony. (Photo by Lewis Bloom)

"That's 'Tonyamato," Schraeger would announce in response to his bandmates' inquiries, as if the new keyboardist's name was one word.

Oeser said he didn't know what to make of the "pain in the ass guy who started showing up all of the time"

"What's this all about?" Oeser asked his band members.

"Don't worry about it," they told him.

Rock-'N-Roll
Cahoots   Rhythm-'N-Blues

Tony Amato/management
775-0323   988-6743

In the beginning, Amato was running sound, serving as the band's manager and joined Cahoots on stage solely for Theiss' originals.

"I just remember it being organic," Oeser said. "Next thing you know his organ is down there in the basement of the rehearsal place and I'm like, I guess we have another player in the band."

Oeser soon became aware of the type of an asset "Tonyamato" would be, with his knowledge of music scene politics and booking requirements. Amato's personality melded perfectly with the band. His pulsating Hammond B-3 thumps and synthesizer lines complemented Michael Scialfa's Fender Rhodes piano and synthesizer style, building upon the catchy melodies of Theiss' songs, the band members recalled.

IN CAHOOTS, IN ASBURY PARK

Some of Cahoots' band members, from left to right, Oeser, Schraeger, Theiss, Scialfa, LaBella and Lursachi in a promotional photo taken in the late 1970s. Amato was not present for the photo.

"The band wasn't really together all that long before Tony became a part of it," Oeser said. "He kind of showed up and we never could get rid of him again."

Cahoots' members continued to rehearse rhythm and blues standards like Eddie Floyd's "Knock on Wood," which they played in previous bands. They breezed through the music of Sam and Dave and vamped a variety of Motown song arrangements. With three powerful singers in Theiss, Oeser and Luraschi, the band was able to pull off the intricate harmonies of Motown music. With a lineup that consisted of two keyboardists and a saxophone player, the band drew comparisons to the

E Street Band. However, its sound more closely resembled the sound of Janis Joplin's final band, Oeser said.

Amato immediately pounded the pavement and got Cahoots through the right doors. He relentlessly networked, searched for gigs, promoted the band and made Cahoots a formidable component of the Asbury Park music scene.

"He was far more integral to our success, at the time, than maybe anybody else in the band," Oeser said. "He had the drive. If he didn't have connections, he made connections. He had a set of balls on him."

The consummate multi-tasker, Amato, was eventually in the studio and on stage with one hand on the mixing board and the other on a nearby keyboard. During the 1970s, all of Asbury Park's clubs required bands to provide their own PA systems. Amato surprised many club promoters by placing the sound board next to his keyboards, so he could simultaneously play and run sound.

"I can't be in two places at once," he would tell promoters who would try to force him into the sound booth.

The Stony Pony even lacked a house system until The Jukes' popularity generated more profits for the club. Cahoots eventually hired its own soundman, Jace Smith and later Lance Larson.

Amato's drive and ambition took Cahoots from Luraschi's basement to The Stone Pony's stage, where the band first opened for Southside Johnny & The Asbury Jukes about one week after its first rehearsal. Amato recalled one afternoon, during which he was approached at The Stone Pony by Van Zandt, who ran the day-to-day operations for Southside Johnny & The Asbury Jukes.

"Where are the boys at? You want a gig?" Van Zandt asked Amato

"When?" Amato replied.

"Tonight," Van Zandt told him.

IN CAHOOTS, IN ASBURY PARK

Amato ran to Luraschi's house on Monmouth Road in Ocean Township, where he found his band mates doing the laundry.

"We've got a gig!" said an excited Amato.

"When?" they asked.

"Tonight. Let's go. Grab your equipment," Amato said.

At the age of 21, Amato was now a professional musician.

"We all packed up and ran to The Pony," he said. "We realized: OK, we're real musicians now."

Amato's persistence earned Cahoots its first show and a weekly slot opening for Southside Johnny & The Asbury Jukes.

"It was great playing for a packed house, that's for sure," said Oeser, about The Stone Pony show.

"The next thing you know, we were off to the races," Schraeger said. "That got us a lot of gigs."

"One Tuesday morning," Amato said. "I get a phone call from Patti Scialfa, Michael's sister, informing me that Michael would not be at the gig Thursday night and that he was taking an extended leave of absence. I called the band up and told them. George comes to my apartment and I learn the rest of the set list. We rehearsed the remainder of the set list for 23 hours straight, slept and then went to the gig opening for the Jukes.

"A year, year-and-a-half goes by, Michael comes back and we're right back where we started."

Chapter 13
A Storm Called Springsteen Strikes

"Bruce wrote from what he knew and what he knew was the Jersey Shore." - Santelli

In October 1975, buoyed by the success of his "Born to Run" (Columbia Records) album, Springsteen and his telecaster simultaneously landed on the front covers of *Time* magazine, where he was hailed as "Rock's New Sensation," and *Newsweek*, on which a teaser in hot pink font read "Making of a Rock Star." *Time* called Springsteen's music "primal," and *Newsweek* boasted similar praise, calling Springsteen "the Real Thing." The magazine covers and success of the "Born to Run" album, which was released in August 1975 and peaked at number three on the *Billboard 200*, created a nationwide buzz and solidified Asbury Park's place on the rock n' roll map. The occurrence became part of a chain of events that gave the city a prominent place in music history. Springsteen wrote the album in his tiny cottage at 7 1/2 West End Court in Long Branch, just around the corner from the Inkwell coffee house.

Carter experienced Springsteen's intensity as he recorded one of the world's most renowned rock anthems, the album's title track. He and Sancious played drums and keyboards respectively on the song, as E Street newcomers Max Weinberg and Roy Bittan performed on the album's remaining tracks. With Springsteen's prolific mind full of ideas, the studio environment was spontaneous and fervent.

"I didn't know what the hell was going on sometimes," Carter said.

Springsteen repeatedly reshaped the song, asking the band members to do multiple takes and pausing numerous times for conferences with his bandmates and the production staff. He kept the entire studio focused on replicating the sound inside his mind, Carter said.

"He was inside himself trying to pull out the best thing he could do," Carter said. "He was very focused on that song, and trying to get it to what he was hearing in his head. I had much respect for him for that."

Even after six takes, Carter was ready for more. He was young, energetic and open to trying the song in different ways. He grew up playing 11 hours per day and was eager to help Springsteen perfect the song. Though many hours had passed, Carter still had fun inside the studio. He and Springsteen started with one idea and experimented with different options before returning full circle to the original Springsteen's first concept.

Carter's years of schooling in the jazz clubs on Asbury Park's west side and early experiences on the road and in the studio had prepared the young musician for this moment. His first paid, professional band was called Little Royal & The Swingmasters. The band played the southern portion of the "chitlin' circuit," which were a collection of clubs in the South, Midwest and eastern U.S. where African-American entertainers performed throughout the 1960s, until racial integration prevailed. The band, whose music was modelled after James Brown, eventually played the East Coast states, such as New York and Florida. For his resemblance to Brown, the band's singer, "Little" Royal Torrance, earned the nickname "Soul Brother Number 2," Carter said.

Carter gained valuable experience of playing with a horn section and driving the rhythm of the band with tasteful drum hits, like a big band drummer. Carter then moved to Richmond, Virginia, where he and Sancious did session work and performed in the band Cinnamon with Tallent. Sancious' friend built Alpha Studios in Richmond, where he and Carter laid down many tracks. Sancious was the first to venture to Richmond and eventually told Carter he should consider moving there. The two shared an apartment in Richmond, performed gigs together and worked at a hospital to stimulate cash flow, Carter said.

"We did anything to survive," Carter said. "It's like our parents taught us."

They focused on establishing themselves in their new hometown, a college town where they hung out with local students and played at the pubs.

"It didn't get too crazy," Carter said. "We were down there to play music and survive."

When Carter wasn't performing or working, he spent most of his time at home practicing on the drums. The main challenge was transporting the band's furniture-sized equipment, including a huge Leslie rotating sound wave speaker, to and from the gigs.

"The two of us hauled this big-ass B-3 organ around," he said. "How the hell we got it up the stairs ... I guess that's youth."

IN CAHOOTS, IN ASBURY PARK

Cinnamon played mainly originals, but Sancious and Carter weren't shy about journeying across new musical avenues and infusing rock, swing, reggae and blues styles into their songs.

Carter stayed in Virginia to do studio work when Sancious and Tallent headed north to play on "Greetings from Asbury Park, N.J." Springsteen and his bandmates spread out and lived in separate Monmouth County communities, which included Asbury Park, West Long Branch and Bradley Beach, Santelli said. They rehearsed in New Jersey and recorded the debut album at 914 Sound Studios in New York, before it was released in January 1973. But listeners in states like Idaho and Montana, who associated New Jersey with the Mafia and pollution, didn't understand the references in Springsteen's songs. The realism of Springsteen's lyrics did not resonate across the states, where places like "Route 88" and "Greasy Lake" might as well have existed on another planet.

"That music was so alien sounding to everybody outside of the Jersey Shore area, because Bruce wrote from what he knew and what he knew was the Jersey Shore," Santelli said.

The band left the Jersey Shore to personally deliver its music to the rest of the country via live shows. The band performed at venues in New Jersey, such as Rutgers University and Monmouth College (now Monmouth University), and then went on its first national tour.

"The only way he has to convince people that what he has to say is valid is through performing," Santelli said. "He realized that very quickly when they saw dismal album sales for 'Greetings' and for 'Wild and Innocent.' That's when the live show took on such significance."

The band knew that its live performances, instead of its recordings, were the only way to show the Nation just how good they were, he said.

The first two singles of Springsteen's debut, "Blinded by the Light" and "Spirit in the Night," failed to appear in the U.S. charts, but Manfred

Josh Davidson

Mann's Earth Band's cover of the latter reached number one on Billboard's Hot 100 in 1977. Springsteen's sophomore release, "The Wild, the Innocent & the E Street Shuffle" (Columbia), sold modestly, but garnered much critical acclaim. The album's only U.S. single, "Rosalita (Come Out Tonight)," became a crowd favorite during live shows for many years.

Eventually, Carter was called and asked to replace Lopez and join The E Street Band on the road. He bounced back and forth between the studio and the road with the band and wound up playing on the title song of Springsteen's third album. "Born to Run" was considered the band's do or die album, due to the modest sales of its two predecessors. The New Jersey references were few and far between on the album, which had more relatable lyrics for audiences outside of the state.

Carter recalled speaking to Springsteen about his experiences in Little Royal & The Swingmasters and some of "Little" Royal Torrance's on stage antics. He told Springsteen how Torrance would throw his hand up in the air as a cue for Carter to hit the snare in synchronization with his hand. As Torrance made quick, simulated karate moves, Carter was expected to accentuate every punch with a drum beat.

"Everything he did, I would do," Carter said.

Springsteen followed suit during his next show, by falling to his knees and expecting Carter to follow along, with each of his drum movements.

"Bruce was open-minded to new things," Carter said.

Carter's experiences in the Swingmasters had also prepared him for the historic moment.

"The energy behind 'Born to Run' was how I played drums," he said. "I was pushing the band, using what I learned in Little Royal's band: how you have to push the band and how you need to drive the band. That is something I learned from Little Royal & The Swingmasters."

IN CAHOOTS, IN ASBURY PARK

The Phil Spector-style "Wall of Sound," which became a signature of the song, eventually buried some of Carter's drum tracks. Having already performed numerous takes, Carter returned to the studio to "pump up" the song's backbeats. He focused intensely on reproducing his drum tracks, with the same passion of the originals.

Lacking today's studio editing tools that can enhance tracks without a musician re-recording them, Carter persistently redid his tracks for each fresh idea. The song launched the mainstream success that Springsteen experienced for the remainder of his career.

"My intention was to drive that song," he said.

After his tour in support of "Born to Run" in 1976, Springsteen filed a lawsuit to sever ties with Appel, who at the time was Springsteen's manager, publisher and co-producer of "Born to Run," so that he could begin to collaborate with Jon Landau. Appel's countersuit led to a Supreme Court injunction that prevented Springsteen from releasing any recordings that didn't include Appel's involvement. Placed on an extended hiatus from recording, The Boss made many frequent, sporadic appearances at The Stone Pony and has done so over the past 40 years.

"He would come down, play with all of the bands, and get drunk," Amato said.

Springsteen brought a buzz to Asbury Park's music scene, which was filled with vibrant musicians.

"I am sure it was very helpful for the Asbury scene to have Bruce roll in whenever he felt like, every once in a while," said Joy Hannan, who dated Springsteen during the hiatus.

The court granted Springsteen the right to choose a new collaborator. He returned to the studio to record "Darkness on the Edge of Town" (Columbia) in June 1977 and released the album one year later. Landau went on to become Springsteen's manager, and co-produce many of his albums.

Josh Davidson

The musicians who performed with Springsteen in Asbury Park learned a lesson to read every portion of a recording contract before signing the dotted line, Hannan said. When he signed the management contract with Appel in his young 20s, Springsteen gave up more control than he had intended, she said.

"I think that was a big eye opener for everybody," Hannan said. "It's fabulous that he came out all right and worked past that and is still doing so well, but it was huge for everybody to see that. They were all innocent. They didn't know the managing part or the business part."

Chapter 14
"Southside" Lays the Foundation

"When Johnny sings about crying, it makes me cry. When he sings about laughter, it makes me laugh…" – Dave Marsh, journalist and current Sirius XM Radio Host

At about 4 p.m. on a rainy Memorial Day in 1976, as lightning fast rollercoasters blared across the tracks and a boardwalk Ferris wheel slowly churned near The Stone Pony, hundreds of anxious fans lined up outside of the club. The marquee announced the live radio broadcast of a party that was held to celebrate the release of "I Don't Want To Go Home" (Epic), the debut album by Southside Johnny & The Asbury Jukes.

"They're the only band worth coming to see 120 times!" exclaimed one fan interviewed outside of The Pony.

Joking with the interviewer, as he stood next to Clemons inside the club, Springsteen said, "What I only want to know is, what are all of you people doing in my town?"

By 10 p.m., more than 1,000 people squeezed inside the club, exceeding the city's fire occupancy ordinance by more than 260. The Jukes opened the show with "Little by Little," a song composed by songwriter/record producer Mel London and made famous by Junior Wells. As the show continued, more than 650 people crowded the surrounding boardwalk, where they listened to Asbury Park's first live concert broadcast.

From center stage Lyon quarterbacked the audience with his rousing chants and bodily gestures, as his bandmates bobbed and swayed to the heart-thumping back beat, crisp guitar strums and seductive horn lines. Kevin Kavanaugh started the Springsteen penned "The Fever," with slow, hypnotizing keyboard notes and chords, followed by The Jukes' sexy, melodic horn runs. Ronnie Spector, who would be inducted into the Rock and Roll Hall of Fame in 2007 with The Ronettes, joined the party for a duet on "You Mean So Much to Me," a song that was written by Springsteen and recorded as the album's final track. Clemons, Bittan and rhythm and blues/pop singer Lee Dorsey, whose songs "Working in the Coal Mine" and "Ya Ya" climbed the Billboard Hot 100 chart in the early 1960s, also performed with the band, before Springsteen participated in the show's finale, which was Sam Cooke's "Having a Party."

"He was just so fantastic tonight," a female fan told the interviewer after the show, regarding Lyon's performance. "I think he is going to be a big star."

"All that I know is that I am making music that I always wanted to make," Lyon told the interviewer at the time.

IN CAHOOTS, IN ASBURY PARK

Members of the record and radio industries and 40 reporters from local newspapers and every major music publications received a live preview of the album, which was released more than a week later.

"I am more excited about Johnny than anything in a long, long time. ... When Johnny sings about crying, it makes me cry. When he sings about laughter, it makes me laugh and that's what makes him great," Dave Marsh, the album review editor of *Rolling Stone*, said at the time. Marsh has since written for *The Village Voice* and *Newsday* and is currently the host of three Sirius XM Radio shows, including "Live from E Street Nation," which airs on E Street Radio.

Springsteen (left) and Lyon (right) share the stage at a benefit for Campanell at The Stone Pony in September 1977. (Photo by Lewis Bloom)

When Robert "Butch" Pielka and John "Jack" Roig opened The Stone Pony on Feb. 8, 1974, no one knew the discotheque would have such a significant impact on rock n' roll. Disco music permeated from the club's speakers for about two years, before the genre began to fade and rock n' roll emerged and reclaimed the Asbury sound. It wasn't long before Southside Johnny & The Asbury Jukes first seized the stage of the club, located on the corner of Second and Ocean avenues, assaulting those same speakers with sexy brass horn lines, soulful vocal serenades and unrelenting melodies. The Jukes were The Stone Pony's first post-disco house band. Eventually, the band's nightly salary was the cover charge, which started at $3, but increased substantially throughout time.

In the mid-1970s, Asbury's musicians brought a New York City style of dress to the Jersey Shore, which was dominated by surfers. Van Zandt donned pink suits, berets and fedora hats. His fellow Jukes wore similar outfits.

"They all looked like pimps," Santelli said. "It was just so urban and so different."

The musicians' sense of style was one of many significant factors that sent a buzz up the East Coast and New Yorkers down the Garden State Parkway to visit The Stone Pony, he said.

"So many things combined to create that scene and take away one or two of them away and the scene might not have happened," he said. "Take them together and they create an incredible buzz and an incredible scene."

The New Yorkers also took notice of the music scene in Long Island and packed rock n' roll clubs, such as My Father's Place, in Roslyn.

At the time, Lyon and Van Zandt were accessible to local audiences, who could drive just a few miles to watch them perform in an intimate Stone Pony setting. Either touring nationally or being confined to the studio, The E Street Band was by then beyond the reach of the Jersey Shore's locals. Fans connected to The Jukes, but their excitement multiplied when Springsteen or his bandmates appeared at The Pony to either listen to or jam with its headlining acts.

IN CAHOOTS, IN ASBURY PARK

"That was the coolest thing about going to The Pony, back then," Santelli said. "There was this sense of excitement. Who was going to play tonight and what were they going to play? A scene evolved from The Jukes and it was not just the music. There was fashion and sensibility. There was a subculture that evolved from it — a Jersey Shore subculture. We all started to dress alike."

It wasn't long before Santelli had a scraggly beard just like Springsteen's and The Pony was packed with men wearing bomber or leather jackets, earrings and news boy caps.

"The scene happened from the music, but then it also touched fashion, sensibility and attitude," Santelli said. "That's why Asbury Park, in some periodicals, was being compared to Liverpool, because it was more than music. There was something else happening that was even bigger than the music, which was the whole culture that the music was energizing."

Fans filled every crevasse of the club during any performance by The Shakes, The Jukes, Cahoots and sometimes The E Street Band. The buzz traveled all the way to Europe, sending an overseas contingent to the venue. The Jukes headlined most nights at The Pony when they were in town. The band's weekly opening acts were Salty Dog on Monday and Fresh on Wednesday. Cahoots and The Shakes took turns opening for The Jukes every Tuesday, Thursday, Friday, Saturday and Sunday. On Sundays, The Jukes led an Upstage-styled jam session.

(left to right) Bobby Buttons, Anson Cooper and Bob Campanell of The Shakes inspire the crowd in 1977 at The Stone Pony. (Photo by Lewis Bloom)

"Everybody would be moving from start to finish," Hector said of The Jukes' performances. "Nobody else was playing R&B at the time. They were like 'The Commitments' (movie about an Irish rhythm and blues band) if you want to make a caricature of it."

During The Jukes' heyday at the club, the band did five 40-minute sets of music with 20 minute breaks in between, Hector said. Half the size it is today, the club was always packed.

"I used to go down to The Pony to see The Jukes a lot," Hector said. "They were a great band. Now when I see them and hear their music it brings me right back to that time. The hot summertime, when they were really doing it. Five sets a night, 20 off, that's tough. That's a long fuckin' night."

The Jukes played many of the electrifying rhythm and blues standards that the rest of the world was starting to forget. Bad Company, The

IN CAHOOTS, IN ASBURY PARK

Rolling Stones and Led Zeppelin shimmied, gyrated and swayed within the stratosphere where Sam Cooke and Wilson Pickett once shuffled their feet. But "horn junkies" like Hannan and hundreds of other fans never failed to pack The Pony and experience the raw, delicate treatment of the rhythm and blues delivered by The Jukes. As some mainstreams artists tried to reinvent funk music, The Jukes continued to play straight up soul.

"(The Jukes) did covers that weren't your average fare," Hector said. "It wasn't 'Black Dog' and it wasn't 'Hotel California.' It was just offbeat stuff, the cool stuff. They were great performers, entertainers and players."

Synchronizing a nine piece rock n' roll band was no easy feat. At rehearsals, Van Zandt orchestrated parts by singing melodies to the horn section, instead of using charts, Hector said.

"They were just different," he said. "There was a void that needed to be filled and you could go into The Pony and hear them do Junior Walker's 'What Does it Take (To Win Your Love)' and you would say, Oh yeah, I love that song! It was just good, fun dance music. They were playing Sam & Dave and shit. Actually, no one else was doing so at that time. There were no other bands playing that style of music, which I knew of in the big club circuit."

They performed every great Sam & Dave song, as well as some blues and many originals. Artists like Boz Scaggs frequently joined The Jukes on stage after performing at Convention Hall.

"Thumper" from The Shakes solos for The Stone Pony crowd in the late 1970s. (Photo by Lewis Bloom)

IN CAHOOTS, IN ASBURY PARK

"Johnny had a great voice," Hector said. "They had a sound. They were young and in their 20s and they rehearsed like motherfuckers. It was real entertainment."

Founded in 1976, The Shakes performed a mix of originals and covers. During the song "Celluloid Heroes" by The Kinks, Bobby Campanell, the band's charismatic lead singer, strolled in place as he sang about walking down Hollywood Boulevard.

"He was just a great performer and he wrote great songs," said Hector of Campanell.

"He has absolutely the sweetest singing voice I have ever heard on a man," Hannan said.

Built around Huey "Piano" Smith's "Sea Cruise," The Shakes' featured rock n' roll medley never failed to engage the audience. Springsteen would occasionally join the party on stage and participate in the medley.

"The Shakes were a solid band, with a lot of stage presence," Hector said. "There was something for everybody."

"They were just amazing," said Joan Cambria, Hannan's best friend and a Stone Pony regular in the 1970s.

The crowd always pleaded for an encore, as soon as The Shakes left the stage. The Shakes would oblige by jumping back on stage and singing The Moody Blues' "Go Now," which begins with the line: "We've already said goodbye."

"I just thought that was hip," Hector said. "I loved the tune."

Lopez performing with Bill Chinnock in 1978 at The Stone Pony. (Photo by Lewis Bloom)

Hector had met The Shakes' drummer, Lopez, when he first arrived in Asbury, but got to know him better through Luraschi.

"Bobby Buttons was a great guitar player. Frank Gross (keyboardist) was solid and also a great singer in his own right and Bobby Campanell was a great entertainer," Hector said.

Steve Lombardelli became the band's saxophone player and keyboardist in 1979. Aside from The Stone Pony, the band performed at New Jersey clubs such as The Dunes in Somers Point and Merals in Margate, and JC Dobbs in Philadelphia, according to its website. The Shakes disbanded for the first time in 1985, before returning in the form of a Campanell and Gross duo in 1988. The full band format returned two years later. Gross, Lombardelli and Carl Fassl, who has also played with the band for many years, lead the present iteration, which performs along the east coast today.

IN CAHOOTS, IN ASBURY PARK

Stir Crazy was another popular Stone Pony house band, with a female lead singer whose voice resembled Pat Benatar's, Hector said.

The Jukes had already packed the club on a nightly basis, before the band requested Cahoots as an opening act.

"Even if the Jukes were out of town, it was still packed," Amato said. "The money was great, but nobody really cared. We wanted to play music."

In the 1970s, bands looked out for and supported one another, sharing things like gigging opportunities and equipment. During the later portion of the era, bands branched out to other East Coast clubs when they weren't performing at The Stone Pony. As Southside Johnny & The Asbury Jukes ventured overseas to England, Cahoots performed at venues along the U.S. East Coast.

"But you had to be back for whatever night you were scheduled at The Pony," Amato said. "Usually, we had Sundays.

Cahoots' debut Stone Pony show with Southside Johnny and The Asbury Jukes marked the beginning of much success for the band. Cahoots opened for many mainstream musicians at The Stone Pony, including Graham Parker and Cheap Trick.

The Stone Pony invites you to its 3rd Anniversary Celebration... Tuesday, February 8, 1977 10 p.m. Featuring... The "SHAKES" and special guests "CAHOOTS" Live on the Radio in A WJLK 1310AM STEREO 94FM Concert Broadcast

Josh Davidson

The Stony Pony has hosted both local and national acts, which had gained prominence in other states and countries. While touring England, Southside Johnny & the Asbury Jukes convinced successful artists such as Graham Parker and Elvis Costello to play at The Stone Pony. Renowned musicians and celebrities visited The Stone Pony after playing at Convention Hall or the casino further along the boardwalk. Amato ran into many celebrities, who dropped in from time-to-time to catch performances by The Jukes or an onstage cameo from Springsteen. The venue's marquee usually included the words "and special guests" under the names of the night's performers in an effort to entice concertgoers with a potential Springsteen appearance.

Lee Mrowicki, the club's disco jockey for decades, recalled Father Fox covering one of Springsteen's songs. He was standing next to Springsteen, as one of the members noticed him watching.

"The guy started freaking out," said Mrowicki. "I just nudged (Springsteen) and said, see what effect you have on people?"

Amato hung out at the back bar with many of the guests, sipping what he and Springsteen had designated as the drink of the summer. Tom Collins, a mixture of lemon juice, sugar, gin and carbonated water received the honor during one summer, while drinks such as Schnapps were chosen in other summers.

"You never knew who you would see," Amato said.

The real "Asbury Sound" era only lasted at The Stone Pony from 1970-1980, Amato said. Then it gave way to what Amato deemed the "Jersey Sound," a completely separate style of music and attitude. Those musicians who made the "Asbury Sound" actually resided in Asbury Park, while those who made the "Jersey Sound," came from areas throughout New Jersey, Virginia, California and other regions of the country. Many of them had never been to Asbury Park in the 1970s and

IN CAHOOTS, IN ASBURY PARK

came to the city with hopes and dreams of being caught in the crossfire of a surprise Springsteen appearance, in which he would hop and stage and share the microphone with them.

"It did happen, but it was OK back then, because everybody wasn't nuts," Amato said.

During its long, storied history, The Pony has hosted an eclectic mix of live bands. The Pony has seen its share of musical styles including new wave, dance, country, metal, blues, R&B, and straight ahead rock n' roll. The spirit and energy that brought the club to life in the mid-1970s has never died.

Chapter 15
In Cahoots, With New Jersey

"Let's not give them a chance to sit down."

Following its first show as the opener for The Jukes at The Stone Pony, it didn't take long for Cahoots to experience an impressive level of success. The music became Cahoots' medicine for the pressure that mounted as a result, but the band also knew how to keep one another amused. Amato was known to surprise his band mates with random acts of nudity.

He couldn't resist the urge to go full monty as he followed behind Schraeger and Oeser in a laundry truck traveling to a gig. The band paid $75 for the truck and used it to transport musical gear. It had a ladder in the back, while the front included storage racks and two removable doors, so a standing driver could be completely exposed to those passing by. Amato closed the truck's side door, took off all of his clothes and pushed the seat back. He honked the horn, reopened the door, and extended his middle finger to his bandmates. As Oeser pulled up in a separate vehicle, he and Schraeger started cracking up and honking the

IN CAHOOTS, IN ASBURY PARK

horn. With his head turned away from the road, Oeser almost crashed the vehicle into a tree in the median of New Jersey State Route 33.

Theiss, left, and Schraeger, right, load equipment into Cahoots' truck at The Stone pony in 1977. (Photo courtesy of Schraeger)

"It was one of the funniest things, I had ever seen in my life," Schraeger said. "It was priceless. This is something you put in a movie."

There were also less public, but equally hilarious episodes of nudity, etched forever in the minds of Amato's bandmates. One time, Amato brought his Cahoots bandmates to the home of Margo and Ronny Harrison, his former bandmates from Brothers and Sisters, so they could record a few songs.

Amato had decided to lighten up the mood after his bandmates became tired and grouchy when they finished recording their first song. It was always a challenge to get his bandmates to loosen up in the high energy, intense pressure studio environment. The band was playing some of Theiss' originals and Amato was playing keyboards in a small glass booth. Schraeger looked up and saw Amato standing naked on a chair.

"All of the sudden, Tony is playing the keyboards and mixing and he's naked, with his ass hanging out through the glass, as we were recording," Schraeger remembered.

Oeser plays percussion in the late 1970s at The Stone Pony. (Photo by Lewis Bloom)

The band members laughed so hard, they had to stop the session. The remaining songs came out great, Schraeger said.

When Cahoots wasn't busy bringing audiences to their feet in Asbury Park, the band traveled up and down the East Coast from Virginia to Connecticut in a 1964 International Bread truck. The band packed clubs and colleges, where they opened for bands like the Monkees. Aside from Monmouth College, where the band drew 3,000 fans and hosted its own radio show, Cahoots played before wild and inebriated students at Trenton State College (now The College of New Jersey), in Ewing, Princeton University in New Jersey and Utica College in New York. With the disco era phased out of the mainstream and rock n' roll and rhythm and blues regaining popularity, Cahoots was also a huge draw at places like New York University in New York City.

"There was a lot of partying going on," Schraeger said. "It was the 70s, man. The cops were partying."

Focused intensely on playing, Cahoots didn't notice it had become a solid draw until a show at the campus tavern of Princeton University.

"There was a line out the door and we said, yeah, hello," Amato said. "We weren't really into that ego bullshit. If you had an ego, we would get rid of you."

Cahoots' band members managed to avoid being arrested during their tenure together, but the band came awfully close one snowy afternoon, as it returned from a gig at Good Time Kates' bar, in Seaside Heights. LaBella, who was driving the truck, noticed sirens in the rearview mirror.

"I don't have my license," Amato recalled him saying.

"I've got my license," Schraeger said enthusiastically.

The band members began to laugh and told Schraeger to hop in the driver's seat, knowing that as the driver, he would be issued the ticket. LaBella pulled the truck over and switched seats with Schraeger. The police officer, who had noticed the truck's lights weren't working, told Schraeger to move the truck, since he was blocking traffic. As the officer walked back to his car, Schraeger said, "I don't know how to drive a stick shift."

"Oh, we're fucked now," LaBella, Amato and Luraschi replied.

Amato had a plan.

"Steve, close the door," Amato told Schraeger.

"For what?"

"Close the fucking door."

Amato leaned over and grabbed the vehicle clutch, while LaBella pushed his foot down on the gas pedal and Luraschi shifted the gears and steered. The team effort to successfully drive the truck around the block resulted in no ticket for Schraeger, who was completely sober.

The band was always too busy to get into trouble with the law, Schraeger said.

"We didn't have any Keith Richards in the band," Amato said. "Well, at least we didn't get caught."

The band was never involved in dangerous activity that could have jeopardized someone else's life and its members were never bailed out of jail. The same went for the other bands in Asbury Park's inner circle.

"People cared about their craft and what they were doing musically," Amato said.

The bandmates frequently hung out together after gigs.

"We caused trouble, but not the kind of trouble that would get us locked up," Amato said.

Luraschi had a tendency to walk off with merchandise that he didn't own. As Cahoots' members set up, Luraschi would sneak off and steal equipment from many venues, Amato said. Luraschi's known thievery first began when he stole the stage lights from Brookdale Community College. At a New York University gig that followed, Luraschi climbed up the rafters to steal more lights. He stole speakers from the famous Strand Theater in Lakewood, New Jersey, which were added to Cahoots' self-built PA system.

Cahoots' band members didn't discover that Luraschi was stealing lights until the New York University gig. As the band set up for its show and the noise level grew quiet, its members heard a socket wrench squeak. Luraschi was on a ladder, removing the venue's stage lights. The band, which didn't own lights, noticed that the collection of lights they were using had become larger than normal. They asked Luraschi if he purchased lighting equipment.

"Oh yeah, I bought more stuff," Amato recalled Luraschi saying.

IN CAHOOTS, IN ASBURY PARK

"Just put them in the truck," Schraeger recalled him saying.

Suddenly, the band's collection of lights had grown.

"John was funny," Amato said. "Nothing was ever nailed down with John."

Returning from a gig with the Monkees at the Rockbox in Somers Point, Cahoots stopped at a gas station. Its owners should have locked down the authentic racing go cart which sat outside. As the band unloaded the truck, the cart was the first thing to fall out.

"What the fuck is this?" Amato asked Luraschi. "What song was this in? Who's going to use this on stage?"

Luraschi's band members never knew which items would magically appear with its gear.

"You would never know what would fall out of the truck, at any given moment," Amato recalled.

Luraschi stole some valuable items, which could have been taken by anyone, since they weren't locked.

"With John, if it wasn't nailed down, be careful," Amato said.

Smaller at the time than it is today, The Stony Pony served as the home base for Cahoots, which played at many other clubs in Asbury Park. There were plenty of opportunities for a band to stay successful without leaving the city. Cahoots amassed an impressive following of fans that came to see them at The Stone Pony after seeing them perform at another New Jersey club. They impressed crowds with their musicianship and energy, rather than their ties to Springsteen.

In New Jersey, Cahoots played at The Royal Manor in Wall Township, The Rock Box in Somers Point, The Rip Tide in Point Pleasant and The Chatter Box in Seaside Heights. Cahoots fans formed huge lines outside of clubs like Trenton State College's Rathskeller, hoping to join the party inside.

"You could fit 1,000 people in there and we did," Amato said. "They weren't coming because they thought Bruce was coming, they were coming to see us. Today, if you go to The Pony, some of the bands that play there will pack them in and play. In real life, they're only packing them in because people are expecting Bruce to show up. So what? He shows, he shows."

As a result of the drinking age lowering from 21 to 18 in 1972, the clubs and college bars were packed with more young and inebriated music fans by the time Cahoots branched out in the mid-1970s. Teenagers traveled from New Jersey's Monmouth, Ocean and Middlesex counties to hear live rock n' roll, disco and disc jockeys. In order to avoid overexposing itself to one venue as it played The Stone Pony on multiples days each week, Cahoots played at venues like Mrs. Jay's, Spanky's and what is known today as The Fast Lane.

"You didn't want to dilute yourself too much," Oeser said.

When it began, Cahoots garnered only a modest income playing about twice per week. The band soon played six to seven nights per week and sometimes multiple venues in one day. Cahoots' schedule loaded up with gigs and the band played shows in New Jersey and throughout the East Coast.

"It was a good time for live music in New Jersey because they had the 18-year-old drinking age. So you had tons of people in the clubs," Oeser said.

At one point, Oeser complained to Amato that Cahoots needed to play more shows. Amato responded by asking one of his agent friends to find more of them.

"Get us what you can," Amato told the agent.

Suddenly, the band was slated to play on 31 straight days before its next day off. Then, it performed 28 continuous shows before taking two days off, followed by another block of 30 gigs.

IN CAHOOTS, IN ASBURY PARK

"By the end of the first month, the lead singer wanted to kill me," Amato said. "The drummer looked at him and said, 'Well, you said you wanted to play more.'"

"I didn't mean this much!" Amato recalled Oeser exclaiming.

Cahoots garnered a lot of buzz in Asbury Park and record labels frequently sent representatives to The Pony to scout the band. They were intrigued by the combination of musical proficiency and on-stage antics which captivated audiences. Partying and enjoying free alcohol became part of Cahoots' routine. With the band members' input, Amato handled most of its business, which included booking. During this era, every club on Asbury Park's boardwalk drew solidly. Fans and record label talent scouts traveled to Asbury Park with hopes of discovering or witnessing the "next big thing." Venues that drew 60 people during Amato's teenage years now brought in at least 100 people. Cahoots and The Shakes consistently drew at least 800 people to its shows, Amato said.

"We built up our name," he said.

Cahoots hired Scott Bigelow, who was born and raised in Asbury Park, as its roadie and security man. Amato would bring the nearly 400 pound future World Wrestling Federation and World Championship Wrestling wrestler, whose nickname became "Bam Bam," on collection runs. The band thought it was a good idea for Amato to bring Bigelow with him to ensure he would come back alive.

"Before we hired him, I had to go collect money with a gun," Amato said.

Bands like Cahoots used their days off to practice, compose and learn new songs. The long nights playing shows and longer hours rehearsing didn't feel like work for the young band, Schraeger said. During the 1970s, band members continued to hang out for about two hours after the clubs closed at 2:30 a.m. They returned home at around 6 a.m., went to sleep and woke up at 2 p.m. They arrived at the venue of their next gig about two hours later for a sound check. Their three set shows started between 8 or 9 p.m.

Cahoots' set list began solely with covers. Eventually, about one-half of its show would include original songs.

"Because if you didn't play covers, you didn't work," Amato said. "Back then if you only did originals you weren't going to play."

Cahoots had an original style of playing music composed by other artists, experimenting with adding cover songs to their set which best fit the band's style. The proficient musicians were even able to try out some blues standards, without the audience heading for the exit.

"We did things our own way," Schraeger said. "We would take a song and add different things to it. We established our own sound."

Throughout their entire careers, each member of Cahoots has played each note of every original and cover song as if it was their last, Oeser said.

"It goes back to getting a song that fits the band and doing it well, doing it like it's the last song you are ever going to sing," he said. "None of us walk through this stuff. We don't mail it in at all. We all have grown up with musicians who have no problem mailing it in. They have no clue on how to delve into their soul to play. There is no emotion or there is a minimal emotion."

The band still managed to butt heads with some club owners. At one point, Pielka threatened to drop Cahoots from the club's lineup if it didn't start learning new material. Pielka continued his rant after the band pointed out that it played four new covers during the week.

"No, no, I want some current stuff," he told them.

Just to bust Pielka's chops, the band jokingly added to its Stone Pony set list Fleetwood Mac's soft rock song "Rhiannon," which was a leap away from the harder-edged rock and rhythm and blues the venue's audiences expected to hear.

IN CAHOOTS, IN ASBURY PARK

Eventually, Cahoots worked through Theiss' soulful, melodic original songs at their rehearsals and they became staples in the band's repertoire. He initiated typical songwriting sessions with the band by singing the lyrics and melodies of his new compositions, while strumming the rhythms on his guitar. Luraschi and Schraeger would chime in with the rhythm section's parts, before Amato added keyboard lines. The rest of the band would join in and a new song was born.

"It was all basement learning," Schraeger said.

Recognizing his knack for stringing together melodies and solidifying song arrangements, Theiss' bandmates tried not to obstruct his talent. Theiss brought his completely composed songs to practice so he could teach his counterparts the chords. He and Amato spent a lot of time fleshing out arrangements before the rest of the band added their parts. Afterwards, Luraschi and Schraeger experimented with a few separate rhythmic feels, Theiss ensured the composition, in its new form, adhered to his original vision and the song took on a new life. Amato impressed Theiss many times during the songwriting process.

"He would play an off chord or something that would just make the whole thing jell," Theiss said. "Even if it wasn't what I thought it was supposed to be."

Theiss' songs were heavily influenced by The Rolling Stones, The Beatles and other 1960s radio artists, who Theiss grew up listening to. Springsteen's influence was noticeable in Theiss' music since the two played together in the Castiles, but Theiss' clearly had a songwriting voice of his own.

During a time when Theiss had paid, extended leave from October through March, he spent the winter staying up late, watching TV and writing songs. One night, the famous crooner, saxophonist and film star Rudy Vallee appeared in a commercial. Theiss composed a song based upon the personas of Vallee and Italian silent film star and legendary ladies' man Rudolph Valentino and the song "Rudy Vallee" was born. The catchy rocker, with a reggae interlude, became one of Cahoots' most popular live songs.

"Rudy Vallee" reminded Theiss of playing "Sidewalks" with the Castiles.

"It's the same thing," he said. "It's a three chord song and it just has the chorus over and over again. People just loved that song and I'm going, I don't get it."

A steady diet of rehearsing and playing live made the band tighter. They decided which songs to keep based on audience reactions during live performances and refined and tweaked those compositions during rehearsals.

"It's a growing process," Schraeger said. "You see what formula works and what doesn't work; what the people like and what they don't like. If you're going to play live, you've got to rehearse."

After Cahoots unveiled a new song, the crowd showed its approval by dancing and cheering. Schraeger was always excited to see the audience members moving their feet to Theiss' grooves and closely listening to the lyrics of his slower ballads.

Oeser witnessed Theiss' transformation from a rhythm guitarist with Doo-Dah to a lead guitar player with Cahoots. Theiss let the saxophone player handle all of Doo-Dah's solos and continued to defer his solos during his early tenure as Cahoots' sole guitarist until he eventually jumped in with leads, Oeser said.

"You've gotta make the horn players earn their money," Oeser joked.

As a band, Cahoots mainly focused on song structure and harmonies, leaving little room for improvisation by its instrumentalists. The band sometimes extended solo sections by four or eight bars, opening up a song for experimentation. The section would become longer when another band member signaled for a solo.

IN CAHOOTS, IN ASBURY PARK

"It was nothing crazy, nothing jazz-like; it was just in the normal cadence of the song," Oeser said.

Sometimes, a band member would notice that the audience's feet were moving more than usual, as a song was ending. The band would continue improvising to keep the song and the audience's enthusiasm alive.

"Let's not give them a chance to sit down," the band member would yell.

Studying other performers, such as The Platters, taught Oeser how to connect with the audience. As an audience member, Oeser always wanted a piece of the joy he witnessed through the large smiles on his musical hero's faces as they swayed to the music on stage.

"You have to go out there smiling," Oeser said. "Go out there like you just got laid and you're going to spread that magical feeling out to everybody. You make your connection with people no matter if there are three, 300 or 3,000 people in the place. You smile the whole time. You want everybody to know what a great time you are having."

Though they occasionally engaged the audience verbally, Cahoots' main focus on stage was its music. Its fans still got to know the band members' personalities, especially after seeing them play repeatedly during the week.

From behind his drum kit, Schraeger drew the audience's attention with his raspy voice during impromptu versions of The Dominoes' "Sixty Minute Man" and ZZ Top's "La Grange."

"That was always great fun," Oeser said of the band's rendition of the ZZ Top song. "He had the voice for it. Out of the band, he was probably the biggest character."

Amato eventually emerged as a character too. Today, he can be found bouncing around the stage or standing behind the keyboard with his hands on hips, exuding a rock n' roll attitude. His on-stage antics in his

60s still include jumping on top of the keyboard, inverting his body and hammering his fingers on the ebony and ivory keys. Still Cahoots and its future iterations have always relied upon the musical proficiency of its band members, rather than their personalities, Oeser said.

In the course of handling the band's business, Amato's experiences were similar to Vinyard's on the New Jersey Turnpike, thanks to Theiss.

"Of course he got jacked up more times for things that I said," Theiss said. "It was another 'please keep your mouth shut' situation, you know."

Theiss would feed Amato things to say to Pielka and Roig, and watch as the two oversized, former-bouncers pressed him against a cigarette machine.

"I would walk in two hours later and they would say, 'Hey George how are you doing?'" Theiss said. "That poor guy. He got a lot of the shit."

Chapter 16
The Calculator

"Steve Van Zandt is 80 percent responsible for the Sounds of Asbury Park and 80 percent responsible for that whole music scene. He created it." - "Boccigalupe"

On a summer night in June, about 30 minutes after performing a midnight set in front of a crowd of 3,000 students at Monmouth College, Amato attempted to enter The Stone Pony. Just as he walked through the door, Roig, the club's owner, grabbed Amato and threw him against a cigarette machine.

"Are you trying to start a war?" Roig asked.

Shortly after, Amato found himself lying on the sidewalk surrounded by glass, after being hurled by Roig through the club's locked door.

Upon investigation, Amato learned that Roig had become infuriated after learning that Cahoots was booked at The Fast Lane (which turned out to be completely untrue). Annoyed at the prospect of losing business, Roig fired the band.

Amato stumbled back to his father's residence and eventually ran into Van Zandt, who lived upstairs.

"Hey, you aren't at The Pony," Amato recalled Van Zandt saying.

Amato spilled the details of the incident.

"Fuck that. Don't worry about it," said Van Zandt, assuring Amato that he would handle the situation.

Amato obeyed Van Zandt's request to keep his lips sealed. Cahoots continued to play shows at other Asbury Park venues, drawing curiosity throughout the city as to why they were prohibited from playing at The Stone Pony.

On the 4th of July, Amato and Schraeger were invited to a barbeque at Springsteen's house. The band shared details of the incident to entertain the party's host and others in attendance, such as Jimmy Iovine, Springsteen's studio engineer at the time, who eventually co-founded Interscope Records; and Patti Smith, a female singer-songwriter who drove the New York City punk rock scene to mid-1970s glory. Meanwhile Cahoots' road crew was setting up for a show at Mrs. Jay's.

Eventually, the band left the barbeque, returned home, changed its clothes and arrived at Mrs. Jay's to help the roadies finish setting up. Cold, Blast and Steel began the night with a reunion show, followed by a set from Cahoots. During Cahoots' set break Amato was told that the entire E Street Band was next door at The Stone Pony. The curious Amato walked over to the club. Skeptical of his business partner's frustration, Pielka let Amato into the club. Upon entering Amato was approached by Obie Dziedzic, a prime assistant for Van Zandt.

"What the fuck are you doing here?" Dziedzic said. "Go back next door."

"Yeah, fine, I'll go back next door," Amato replied.

IN CAHOOTS, IN ASBURY PARK

Amato turned and walked out the door. As he walked the sidewalk on his way back to Mrs. Jay's, Amato noticed the surprised gazes of several onlookers.

"What the fuck's wrong with them?" he thought.

Amato turned his head and noticed that Dziedzic and the entire E Street band was behind him in single file. The band and its entire audience had filed out of The Pony and began to follow Amato on his way to Mrs. Jay's.

"What the fuck?" he thought.

Before he knew it, Amato was in a blocked off area in back of Mrs. Jay's, where members of Cahoots and The E Street Band merged. Amato was designated the tambourine player, while Federici played the organ. Michael Scialfa and Van Zandt were the guitarists and Bittan handled the keyboards.

"We had the whole E Street Band and Cahoots on the small fuckin' stage," Amato said. "The only person who wasn't there was Bruce, because he couldn't be involved in this one."

Onlookers hung over the fence in the back of the club, hoping to catch a glimpse of the action.

"They had to block off half of Ocean Avenue, because it was nuts," Amato said. "The place was mobbed all over. There were people standing in the kitchen area where they cook."

After playing a few songs, Amato felt Van Zandt nudge him.

"Look, out there," Van Zandt said.

Amato noticed the 6'7" Roig and 6'2" Pielka glaring at him with their arms folded. The oversized, former bouncers were enraged that the only person left in their club next door was one bartender designated to watch to the cash register.

"Boy, you're going to get your ass kicked now," said Van Zandt as he laughed.

It took about an hour to clear out the club after the 90-minute set. The entire E Street Band moved to Mrs. Jay's beer garden where they drank pitchers of beer. After walking over with his drink, Amato heard a voice from a dark, nearby corner.

"Hey Tony, can we talk to you?" he heard Roig say.

Amato shot a look in Van Zandt's direction and said, "Well, fuck that,"

"Hey, Clarence, you wanna come with me?" Amato asked "Big Man" Clemons.

"No, you are on your own on this one, brother," Clemons responded.

Finally, he convinced LaBella, who is even smaller than him, to share the moment.

"That's the only guy that had the nuts to come over with me," Amato said.

Amato and LaBella nervously approached the two club owners, who had a reputation for beating people up and sometimes pulling a gun. They had already thrown Lopez through a wall, Amato said.

"First off all, I'd like to apologize," said Roig, as a chorus of beer mugs dropped to the table where the members of The E Street band were sitting. "How can we get you back into The Pony?"

"Oh no, here goes this motherfucker now," Van Zandt said from the other side of the room.

"Well, we would like to have our steady nights back and we'd like to have a raise," Amato said.

"Don't worry. Done. No problem," said both club owners.

"And, by the way, we need a new PA."

"How much do you need?"

"$2,500"

"Done. No problem."

IN CAHOOTS, IN ASBURY PARK

The table full of E Street Band members broke out into laughter, as Amato returned.

"How the fuck did you do that without getting killed?" they asked.

"I don't know," he responded.

The mutual respect between Cahoots and The Stone Pony's owners diffused the situation. Amato also learned the band-merging event at Mrs. Jay's was orchestrated by The E Street Band, who felt Cahoots had been treated unfairly. Despite what Roig believed, Cahoots was never asked to play The Fast Lane in the first place.

"(The E Street Band members) knew where we were," Amato said. "They had no business going in The Pony. They just did that to empty the club out. Steven (Van Zandt) was the guy who planned it, because Steve planned everything. Steven was the great calculator. Steve Van Zandt is 80 percent responsible for the Sounds of Asbury Park and 80 percent responsible for that whole music scene. He created it."

Pielka and Roig started a war, but couldn't win due to the strong bond between the bands, Amato said.

"The E Street band respected us. We respected them. We were all a family," he said.

Pielka and Roig were equal members of the brotherhood.

"They were included because we're all family and in a family you have fights," Amato said.

"That one just worked out in my favor."

Still, it was never a good idea to rub either of the club owners the wrong way.

"They're nice guys, but you wouldn't want them mad," Schraeger said.

"They were tough guys," Amato said. "You don't fuck with them."

Schraeger remembered repeated occasions when Springsteen and Van Zandt called Amato's house after similar incidents to ensure he was OK.

"They were always looking out for him and us," Schraeger said.

"They cared, it was a brotherhood," Amato said.

Van Zandt was a mentor who taught Amato important lessons on the music business and Asbury Park music scene. Van Zandt and Springsteen were instrumental in helping the Stone Pony house bands reach the next phases of their careers, Amato said.

"You can't talk about the Asbury music scene or the Jersey thing at that time, in that era without mentioning Bruce Springsteen and Steve Van Zandt. ... They had a lot of input into our bands," Amato said. "Steve helped The Shakes. Bruce helped Cahoots. That's the way it was.

It all started from Bruce Springsteen, but Van Zandt was the catalyst for The Jukes."

Van Zandt was born in Massachusetts on Nov. 22, 1950, and moved to Middletown Township at the age of 7. Before founding The Jukes, Van Zandt performed with the Dovells, a white vocal group that experienced minor success in the early 1960s. After leaving The Jukes to join The E Street Band, Van Zandt continued to play a role in guiding his former band on its successful path. He joined The E Street band in 1975, but continued as songwriter and producer for his former band. He left the E Street Band in 1984 and released a number of solo albums, some which were politically charged, before returning permanently to the E Street Band in 1995.

During one of Springsteen's summer parties in 1999, Theiss was sitting across from Van Zandt, who appeared to be in a depressed mood, as he pondered the next move of his career. Van Zandt told Theiss he had an audition for a show on HBO, but wasn't sure what to do.

"And then he's on 'The Sopranos' and that's a fucking hit," Theiss said. "That's the way shit goes down all of the time."

Though an entertainer may not be sure where their career is headed, the next week they might find themselves on one of the most successful and critically acclaimed cable television shows in history. With no acting

IN CAHOOTS, IN ASBURY PARK

experience, Van Zandt joined the show's cast as Silvio Dante, the right hand man of the program's main character, Tony Soprano.

Chapter 17
Joy, Joan & the Asbury Fans

"The noise was so physical. You just breathed it in and you could feel your blood racing." – Joy Hannan, fan

Joan Cambria and Joy Hannan were a couple of bored college students hanging out at Hook Line & Sinker in Rumson, New Jersey, during summer break, before they experienced the profound impact The Stone Pony had on the Jersey Shore's youth in the 1970s. Unsatisfied with the bar scene or lack thereof in their hometown of nearby Little Silver, they decided to head for greener pastures.

"Oh my god, really, is this all there is?" Hannan asked Cambria. "There's got to be something better than this."

"There is more," Cambria replied. "There is life outside of Rumson."

IN CAHOOTS, IN ASBURY PARK

(left to right) Hannan and Amato share a laugh in the late 1970s. (Photo courtesy of Hannan)

They decided to leave their wild child friend, Jeanine, behind in the tame Rumson scene and follow the suggestion of Hannan's co-worker, Judy DeNucci, and drive to The Stone Pony. Hannan and DeNucci worked together as cocktail waitresses at Rosie O'Grady's in Eatontown. Jeanine was content with the convenience of being thrown out of bars near her house, while Hannan and Cambria wished to expand their horizons.

"She wanted to be a wild child in the calm pond and we wanted to be the calm people in the wild pond," Hannan said.

The next night, Cambria and Hannan were standing in The Stone Pony where the house band, Southside Johnny & The Asbury Jukes, were shaking, rattling and rolling, before they became stars. The female-fronted hard rockers, Heart, were performing across the street at Convention Hall. It was a night they would never forget and one that would forever alter their lives.

The women made many repeated trips to The Pony. From the quiet street, Hannan would approach The Pony's entrance where a completely different world awaited inside. Once the door opened, one was struck by a lightning fast metamorphosis of heart thumping, excruciatingly loud music. Without hesitation, she left her troubles outside and danced the night away.

"You would go into another world," Hannan said. "Once the door opened, you experienced that shock of noise and everything else that just would hit you. It was almost a physical force."

Music pulsated through the club's speakers that changed one's state of body and mind.

"You could feel your heart change rhythm," Hannan said. "The noise was so physical. You just breathed it in and you could feel your blood racing."

As mainstream music grew stale, Asbury Park was a place where the self-professed "horn junkie" could get her fix. The club's first house band, Southside Johnny & The Asbury Jukes, consistently delivered mind blowing performances until the early morning hours. After The Jukes started to pack the house, other house bands like Cahoots, The Shakes and Salty Doug were added to the mix.

"Cahoots definitely was one of the best house bands," Hannan said.

The band always sounded tight, said Cambria, who briefly dated Amato.

"They used to play a lot of just fun rock n' roll songs, interspersed, all of the time," she said.

IN CAHOOTS, IN ASBURY PARK

(right to left) Amato jumps into Hannan's arms, as Cambria (front) watches during the CD release party for Boccigalupe & the Badboys' "Never Needed Anyone" at Tim McLoone's Supper Club, Asbury Park, in 2013.
(Photo taken by Conni Freestone)

Hannan recalled picking up Amato and throwing him over her shoulder, upon first meeting him.

"He was just the cutest person in the world. I used to carry him around," she said.

"He was funny, sweet and sincere," Cambria said. "He was just a good, honest and open person."

After graduating college in 1976, Cambria and Hannan drove from Little Silver to The Pony more frequently. One year later, Hannan who had focused on visual arts and Cambria who had a performance arts background both shared a one bedroom apartment on 8th Avenue in Asbury Park.

Josh Davidson

"We made the living room into the second bedroom, so we used to call The Stone Pony our living room," Cambria said. "That was before The Pony had its second back room and that room is what Butch and Jack called 'the room that Southside built,' because it was his revenue that allowed them to purchase it."

The pair, who were best friends since the sixth grade, moved to 2nd Avenue shortly after being robbed. Both women became part of the circle of closely bonded friends in the Asbury Park music scene. At The Pony, when Pielka saw Hannan he would stick out his muscular arm and flip her over. Defying the laws of gravity, Hannan's drink always remained comfortably in her hand. Many times, Hannan stood on a chair when speaking with Roig, so she could communicate at an eye level with the giant man.

Cambria described Pielka and Roig as sweethearts.

"They were fabulous," Hannan said. "They were always really, really sweet to us."

When Hannan dated Springsteen, she and DeNucci, who dated Pielka, were always followed by enormous bouncers as they wreaked havoc on the venue and earned the nickname the "untouchables." Any men who dared to talk to them were no sooner intimidated by the oversized bouncers who crept up behind the two women. Fearing a tussle with a bouncer twice their size, the men would stutter the words "bye, bye," Hannan said.

"We wreaked havoc in The Pony, because we had these enormous bouncers Eric and Carl right behind us," she said. "If we were just doing whatever we were doing and a guy started talking to us, soon enough one of them would be standing over one of our shoulders. We could do whatever we wanted. It was great. I never had such power."

When Springsteen jumped on stage and a large mass of people charged forward, the bouncers stood in a line parallel to the stage and

IN CAHOOTS, IN ASBURY PARK

locked arms to keep the crowd back on the dance floor. Hannan and DeNucci stood between the stage and the bouncers' interlocked arms, which served as a human fence to protect both women.

In the 1970s, Springsteen and his comrades from Asbury Park found their idols like Gary U.S. Bonds and Ronnie Spector — whose popularity had long since waned — and helped them rebuild their careers.

"That group of musicians actually helped the musicians before them," Hannan said.

On one night Springsteen went to a dive bar across the street from The Pony to take in a performance by Bonds, a rock n' roll/rhythm and blues singer, whose song "Quarter to Three," had reached number one and sold more than a million copies in 1961.

"It was the only time you ever saw Bruce get drunk, because he was so upset," Cambria said. "He said, 'Look what happened to his career. What if this happens to me?'"

Bonds' career eventually turned around quite impressively.

One night Springsteen and some other Asbury Park musicians walked into a bar where they found Spector, who clearly needed support.

"I remember Bruce telling me she looked like the devil and sounded like an angel," Hannan said.

The musicians pulled Spector out of obscurity and reinvigorated the career of the onetime star of the early 1960s, who had already scored mega hits like "Be My Baby" and "Baby, I Love You."

On The Pony's stage the animated musicians playfully fed off one another, making faces at each other and dancing with their counterparts as they played. Their energy fed directly into the audience until the entire club was electrified.

"They were having as much fun on the stage as we were on the dance floor," Hannan said.

Josh Davidson

Fans were treated to many impromptu performances by musicians from other bands who joined their friends on stage. The number of musicians rapidly multiplied until most of the stage was covered. The lyrics and instrumentation of each cover song evolved into a much different composition than the album version.

"One band would be playing and if there was another musician in the crowd, they would just get on stage," Hannan said. "It would just multiply until any of the musicians that happened to be walking around in the bar were on stage."

During one night, Cambria and Hannan watched from the orchestra pit of the local Ritz-Carlton as Springsteen filled in for Lyon, who had fallen ill. "Miami" Steven Van Zandt, as he was known at the time, brought 10 "Miami Horns" players to the stage and the oversized rock orchestra made the audience blissful.

"It was incredible," Hannah said. "There were probably 30 people on stage. I will never forget that concert."

The two women still watch local bands in Asbury Park and even sometimes in Rumson. Recently, Hannan and Cambria attended a performance by local musicians Lee Howard and Bob Burger in Rumson and became frustrated as the younger attendees carried on a conversation, not paying attention to the music.

"They had to yell to be heard over the great music they were ignoring," Hannan said.

"So how do you like the music?" Cambria yelled to Hannan in exaggerated and mocking voice, hoping the people would get the hint. They didn't.

"They were missing out," Hannan said. "They had no clues as to who was singing and what a good job they were doing. It's a shame."

Chapter 18
The Souvenir

"These guys were serious about their music and serious about the fidelity of the music and that came through. It kept you wanting to go back." – Ray Maxwell, fan, regarding Cahoots

During one night at The Pony in the late 1970s, Springsteen was standing near the men's room, leaning up against the wall and sipping a drink, when a customer asked waitress Lisa Ferrara to see if he could take a photo or sign an autograph. Ferrara told the patron she would do so for $10.

After approaching The Boss, Ferrara told him it would only be fair if he kept the $10. She joked that they could make an impressive profit by charging each of The Pony's customers for Springsteen souvenirs.

Springsteen looked at Ferrara, laughed and said, "Liz, don't worry, you keep it."

Springsteen obliged the request and Ferrara made $10.

Before taking the place of a waitress who had quit her job at The Stone Pony in 1976, the 21-year-old Ferrara was employed at Canadian Furs and Fashions, which was located across the street from Steinbach's department store on Cookman Avenue. She started by working at the fur store by day and waitressing at the Stone Pony at night. She lived in an apartment with no furniture on Asbury's 8th Avenue. At Canadian Furs and Fashions, Ferrera was a firsthand witness to the disco invasion of the resort shore city. Women came in and bought disco dresses and high heel shoes for disco nights at the nearby Stone Pony. Transvestites purchased clothing for performances at the city's venues.

Disco acts still performed weekend gigs at The Stone Pony, by the time Ferrara became a full-time waitress. But Roig and Pielka eventually phased out disco and completely focused on rock. As the club gained popularity, Ferrara spotted numerous movies stars and musicians such as Ronnie Spector in the club. Members of the E Street appeared frequently. When Ferrara simultaneously spotted three E Street Band members at the club, she knew an on stage appearance was imminent. The band used The Pony to try out new material before embarking on one of its world tours, Ferrara said. Even when The E Street Band wasn't in town, the club was packed with Springsteen fans expecting a sporadic stage appearance by The Boss.

When the E Street Band's members weren't playing at the club, they usually came in separately. Clemons and Weinberg frequented the club and hung out at the back bar. Federici usually brought a friend with him. Tallent and Bittan visited the venue less frequently.

IN CAHOOTS, IN ASBURY PARK

Ferrara worked Monday nights so she could take in a performance by Stir Crazy, whose singer sounded exactly like Janis Joplin. She also enjoyed watching the heavy metal band Salty Dog.

"I loved them," she said. "I used to actually follow them around."

Roig and Pielka were both pleasant and fair employers, but Pielka was more personable, Ferrara said. Pielka interacted more with the Stone Pony team, since he was at the club from opening to closing, she said. Roig showed up for meetings and occasionally spent time walking throughout the club, sitting and talking with the concertgoers. Each year the club would host a party for its bartenders and the staff would split the proceeds.

"They were really good to us," she said.

Pielka always let the staff know where they stood and didn't harp on any issues, Ferrara said. He pointed out both the positives and negatives to them.

"Butch was very straight forward," Ferrara said. "He would never pull any punches."

Pielka did not frown upon bar patrons purchasing drinks for the staff, Ferrara said.

"It was a party atmosphere and nine times out of 10 when we were working, we were drinking," she said.

During one night, Pielka pulled Ferrara and two other staff members aside and asked them to quietly and discreetly peak under the venues' tables and chairs. As the covert operation proceeded, under Pielka's command, none of the patrons knew that the club had received a bomb threat. Under the same circumstances today, the club would have been evacuated rapidly, Ferrara said.

Most of Asbury Park's musicians, like the hilarious and laid-back keyboardist Paul Venier of Salty Dog, treated The Pony's bartenders very well, Ferrara said. Venier is now a comedian who is well-known, especially in New Jersey. The band members and Pony staff spent many hours hanging out after the club closed. During summer weekends, many big name artists headed to the Pony after performing at Convention Hall. Pielka and Roig locked the doors for a private show, until 3 or 4 a.m., with The Pony's headliner for the night. On many occasions, Convention Hall headliners like Tom Petty and Hall & Oates joined them on stage. On other nights, the staff hung out together, ate, drank and sometimes headed to another restaurant after the bar closed. Ferrara would stay until 6 or 7 a.m., go home, get into her bathing suit and head to Asbury's beach.

As The Jukes' notoriety increased, space on the dance floor became a treasured commodity.

Barely able to flex a muscle, the young men and women crowded the front of the stage and gazed at the excitement before them.

"When The Jukes became more famous and more people were coming, it was to the point where nobody could even dance anymore," Ferrara said. "It was crowded. I could barely even get through to bring drinks to the table. It was insane."

Rich Kelly, a local music fan who lived in Belmar, experienced The Jukes before they were notorious for shaking The Stone Pony's walls. In his early 20s and working as an Army civilian at New Jersey's Fort Dix, Kelly saw the band perform in its previous life as The Blackberry Booze Band, beginning in 1974. Kelly and his co-workers watched the band at The Pony until 1 a.m. every Tuesday, Thursday and Sunday, before waking up a few hours later and driving 40 miles to work.

"They were just playing these great songs," Kelly said. "They performed rhythm and blues and soul music in their own way. They were really talented."

Kelly made his first trip to The Pony after a friend found him spending a Sunday night in the Empire Bar, a tiny dive nearby, whose

IN CAHOOTS, IN ASBURY PARK

main form of entertainment was a bumper pool table. The friend told Kelly about the great music found inside the newly opened Stone Pony. It wasn't long before Kelly and his friends frequented the venue in search of girls, beer and music. Modest crowds watched The Blackberry Booze Band until the band's members traded in their t-shirts and jeans for polyester pants, blazers and fedora hats and packed the club as Southside Johnny & The Asbury Jukes.

The Blackberry Booze Band and The Jukes introduced Kelly, who grew up on British rock, to a new world of music. He attended The Pony religiously and spent some of his free time researching the artists covered by its house band, such as Jimmy Cliff and Solomon Burke.

"When I started hanging out and watching the Jukes, I just got a whole new perspective on a different style of music that I had never heard before," Kelly said.

When The Jukes began to tour other parts of the world, Kelly and his friends enjoyed listening to and watching The Shakes and Cahoots.

(left to right) "Thumper," Buttons, Campanell and Cooper of The Shakes in 1977 at The Stone Pony. (Photo by Lewis Bloom)

"I really liked Cahoots," Kelly said. "The Shakes were not only a good band, their lead singer, Bobby Campanell, was a very funny guy and a great entertainer."

Kelly also watched bands perform at Mrs. Jay's and One Sane Man. On the weekends he saw bands such as The Doors, Jefferson Airplane, Chicago, The Eagles, Yes and Grand Funk Railroad at Convention Hall until 1978, when his visits to Asbury Park gave way to other interests, such as marathon running.

Driving past neighboring Bradley Beach into Asbury Park, Ray Maxwell, a local fan in his mid-20s, became keenly aware of the abandoned homes and emptiness of his surroundings. He could see the lights emanating from The Pony, as his car approached the ocean. By the late 1970s, the city had changed drastically since Maxwell's days as a Belmar youth.

"It was really a surreal experience going there at the time," Maxwell said.

When cars filled the club's parking lot with a popular headliner on stage, Maxwell had to park at least three blocks away. Nervous about the possibility of having his car stolen or damaged, Maxwell entered the club and his worries were forgotten.

After visiting his family at the Jersey Shore for the weekend, Maxwell and friends, including Kelly, would stop at The Pony to catch the headliners' first set every Sunday. Come 2 a.m., Maxwell was still at the club, enjoying the band, without focusing on the fact that he needed to return in a few hours to Manhattan, where he lived and worked.

"Once you went into the club, you didn't think of the time," Maxwell said.

Most of the fans' attention spans were planted on the opposite sex.

IN CAHOOTS, IN ASBURY PARK

"The guys were there to pick up the girls and hear the music," Maxwell said. "The girls were there to pick up the musicians. There were always plenty more girls than musicians, so we all had fun."

The club was packed by midnight and stayed open well beyond the 2 a.m. closing time, mandated by the city. At 2:45 a.m., when the club announced last call, its patrons would crowd the bar and order a dozen beers per person, so they could extend their fun, Maxwell said.

"Then you would sit there and you would drink, until the sun came up," he said.

Uttering the words, "I did it again," the patrons somehow made it through rush hour and to their desks for work.

The bands kept the audience engaged by playing multiple sets without dillydallying between songs. Some songs stuck with Maxwell and he would wait for the bands to play them. The Shakes teased the crowd, as it anticipated the original song "Jersey Reggae," only to be told it would be played next set.

The Shakes and Cahoots mastered the art of covering songs from the prior decade without trying to duplicate the album versions, Maxwell said. Maxwell connected with the music the headliners replicated, since they were the songs that dominated his teenage years.

"I think that's what kept everybody coming back," he said.

Cahoots opened many nights with a Motown medley, which started with "Back in My Arms Again," by The Supremes. The band started the song by whacking an up tempo count on a cowbell. The highlight for Maxwell was hearing the band harmonize during the chorus.

"When they hit those harmonies, it was just magic," he said. "That was the first song of the night and it just rolled from there."

Oeser had a great voice and knew how to work the crowd, Maxwell said.

"He could sing anything," Maxwell said. "Whatever song they put at him, he could do it."

He also never seemed phased or intimated when famous singers, like Springsteen and Lyon, joined Cahoots on stage. Oeser and his bandmates skillfully kept the crowd engaged.

"These guys just had that ability to fill a room and get everybody involved," Maxwell said. "Even if you were having a sidebar conversation with somebody, the music was what was drawing you there."

Maxwell sometimes enjoyed the Stone Pony bands' first sets the most, since that is when they performed original music. Cahoots wrote great songs, which contrasted greatly from the jingly pop that was performed by some of the era's mainstream acts, Maxwell said.

"They kind of had that sort of edgy rock, we're in Asbury kind of vibe to it," Maxwell said. "These guys were serious about their music and serious about the fidelity of the music and that came through. It kept you wanting to go back."

Cahoots, which Maxwell has seen about 30 times, successfully blended various styles of music into a rhythm blues, Motown-based sound, he said.

"Their harmonies were just so tight," he said. "They really honed that craft of singing."

Maxwell attended high school with Luraschi and graduated one year prior to him. The two had lost track with one another for a few years, before becoming reacquainted at The Pony. Luraschi was a quiet, nice person, Maxwell recalled.

"If you met him off stage, you just wouldn't believe he was the guy up there," he said.

From the stage, Luraschi would wave to Maxwell, upon seeing him. During set breaks, Luraschi sat with Maxwell and his friends and caught up on old times.

IN CAHOOTS, IN ASBURY PARK

"It's a big deal when one of the guys from the band actually comes down to your table and sits with you for a few minutes," Maxwell said. "I always remembered and respected that. It was real nice of him. He never got too big in his fame. He had a good run with his music, but it never changed the core, nice guy that he was all along."

Maxwell was impressed by the respect the musicians displayed when sitting in with the headlining acts. Members of The Jukes or E Street Band who jammed on stage with Cahoots never tried to upstage them.

"Springsteen would never try and take the show away from Johnny; Johnny would never try to take the show away from Cahoots," Maxwell said. "If they ever needed an extra horn, the guy from the Miami Horns would never try to overplay, he would just play, and that's why it worked so much."

During one Sunday night at The Pony when Lyon was unavailable, Van Zandt took center stage for The Jukes' performance. The band shifted its repertoire and played a set list tailored for Van Zandt's style. Shifting gears, The Jukes began the show with "Papa's Got a Brand New Bag" by James Brown.

"And it was great, "Maxwell said. "It wasn't the night you were expecting, because you were kind of used to Johnny's set, but he just opened with a completely different vibe and then the show was crazy from there."

The Jukes were a solid attraction on any night.

"Johnny was a good singer and he really knew how to play off the Miami Horns," Maxwell said. "There was just a real tightness of the band."

Van Zandt always seemed to enjoy playing the most and could never wait to get on stage, Maxwell said. He skillfully drew and played off of the musicians who were around him.

"He made everybody better, just because he was such a good musician," Maxwell said.

The Shakes' stage presence and quirkiness made them stand out on stage, Maxwell said. They never disappointed the fans who waited for them to perform "Ain't That Peculiar," by Marvin Gaye.

"The way they did that song was just always good," Maxwell said. "You knew they were going to do it and as soon as they hit the first few bars, you knew that was it. The way that they would do that song would always entertain you."

The Shakes managed to slowly build its fan base at The Pony. Beginning as an unknown, the band started drawing increasingly larger crowds after just a few weeks, Maxwell said. In just two months, The Shakes' draw was similar to Cahoots' fan base.

"That was a pretty big jump," Maxwell said.

Pielka and Roig were astute businessmen who understood the importance of booking solid bands during weeknights, when drawing a crowd was more of a challenge. They placed less emphasis on booking a solid drawing band for the weekend, when filling the club was easy, Maxwell said. They made visiting the club a positive experience with quality and prompt service, he said.

Rumors of a Springsteen appearance were spread to draw audiences when business was slow, but audiences didn't go just to hear Springsteen, Maxwell said. Fans went to The Pony to see the headlining act and the special guests were only a bonus. With 20 musicians packing the stage on occasion, Maxwell always knew the night would get even better when guest musicians arrived.

Playing in the close confines of The Stone Pony, where room was sparse between the band and stage, bands had to treat its audience as part of the show, he said.

IN CAHOOTS, IN ASBURY PARK

"The intimacy of it was very special," Maxwell said. "You could reach out and touch the bands from almost anywhere in the club."

Many times, in the mid-1960s, a 7-year-old Tim "Squeaky" O'Neill and his sister climbed up a garbage can outside of the Vinyard's residence, hung through a window and watched The Castiles' rehearse. The two siblings marveled at the young band's ability to make real music.

By early 1975, O'Neill stood on Ocean Avenue, just outside of The Stone Pony, watching throngs of people assemble around the club and enter its doors. He was only able to observe from the outside until, finally, a local singer snuck the 16-year-old inside.

Taken under the wing of Asbury Park regulars like Amato, Luraschi and Schraeger, O'Neill became familiar with scene shortly after first entering The Stone Pony. O'Neill, who had just run away from home, received a warm welcome from the three Cahoots members, who were a few years older than him.

"Steve Schraeger was the first guy in the Asbury music scene who made me feel at home," O'Neill said. "I guess he looked at me like I was some little kid or something, but he always made me feel like I belonged there."

It wasn't long before Cahoots made O'Neill feel like part of the band. Off stage, the band's members spent most of their moments together, joking around and laughing, O'Neill said. The fun and energy followed them on stage and spread itself throughout the audience.

"It always felt good when those guys were playing," O'Neill said.

Still a fan on the outside looking in, like the 7-year-old staring into the Vinyard residence, O'Neill longed to hear the music of Asbury Park. He started to work the door at The Pony, after The Jukes went on tour, following their debut album. On stage, the musicians enjoyed each moment so intensely that they probably didn't notice they were becoming part of a historical scene, O'Neill said.

From the audience, O'Neill watched as Schraeger stared intensely at the audience, as he concentrated completely on playing music. As his head whipped back and forth, Amato masterfully played the role of maestro and lead the band and audience with his animated facial and bodily expressions. Luraschi stood comfortably in front of his gear and consistently laid down solid grooves, O'Neill said.

"He would get up on the stage, put his bass on, plug it in and he felt right at home," O'Neill said. "It seemed like everything that he did was just effortless. He was the embodiment of a rhythm section. He was a great tempo keeper."

With Schraeger's beat behind Luraschi's thump, O'Neill witnessed the inception of a rhythm section that would play a major role in defining the Asbury Park music scene.

"Any band those guys were in, the rhythm section kicked ass," O'Neill said. "I really believe that the Asbury sound stemmed from guys like that. People think of The Jukes and they think of Springsteen, but the real Asbury Park sound, at least from 1973-1979, I think it was based on those guys."

Each night, bands like the Shakes and Cahoots made Asbury Park a hub where musical expression flowed freely. The bands' members lived what would become a piece of rock n' roll history, but their music never crossed into the mainstream.

"It's such a shame that they never latched onto some vehicle that really made it worth their while, but they were the survivors," O'Neill said.

O'Neill noticed the camaraderie among the tightly knit community of Asbury Park musicians and eventually became a part of the brotherhood.

"Whenever I roll through Asbury Park now, those are the visions in my head," O'Neill said. "The days of The Pony and Steve, Tony, John Luraschi – all those guys. There were a lot more (musicians), not just

IN CAHOOTS, IN ASBURY PARK

them. Those guys, the three of them, I would say those were the staples for me. They were like my big brothers and even though they are like two feet shorter than me, those guys were a couple of years older than I was and I loved being around them. I learned a lot about music and I learned a lot about people."

Chapter 19
"That Son of a Bitch"

"The drinks were flowing until about 6 a.m. when Lance Larson, an Asbury Park singer/guitarist, announced, 'We're all out of beer.'"

As he and two fellow members from the Salty Dog road crew walked from the band house to Hunter Village, O'Neill noticed a small, white box truck stuck in the snow, on the wrong side of the two lane road at Hunter Mountain, in Lanesville, New York. From a distance, O'Neill noticed a group of men hovering around the vehicle, unsuccessfully trying to push it out. As he walked closer, O'Neill noticed one of the men was wearing an oversized hat with its brim pulled down on one side. A fashion statement for some, this was the sanctioned headgear for an Asbury Park musician. Like he needed any more proof, the raspy shrill of Schraeger's voice sealed the deal. Cahoots had arrived at Hunter Mountain.

"We're stuck in the snow," Schraeger told him. "We can't get the truck out."

With his brothers in need of help, O'Neill turned to his fellow crew members and said, "Hey man, these are my family, we've got to do this."

"Absolutely man, let's do it," they replied enthusiastically.

After a few minutes of attempting to push the truck, they realized the only way to release the truck from its purgatory was to unload the equipment inside. O'Neill and the crew were used to loading and unloading the enormous sound system, PA, light show and stage equipment for the well-established Salty Dog on a nightly basis. So they expected unloading the equipment from the small truck would be a piece of cake. The group of men successfully unloaded the equipment into the club where Salty Dog would perform later that evening. The vehicle drove away comfortably in the correct lane.

With a relentless work ethic, Cahoots was no stranger to fun on and off of the stage. In 1977, during its first gig at Hunter Mountain, Cahoots joined its East Coast counterparts, Salty Dog and Salvation, for a weekend of gigging and debauchery.

"You don't want those three bands up there at one time, because Hunter Mountain or the hotel we were staying in would never be the same," Amato said.

On a Thursday night, Amato, Schraeger and Cahoots' roadie Larry "Bozo" Blasco rented a truck and headed north to the ski resort. The three men stunned Salty Dog by showing up unannounced to its show. The rest of Cahoots' band members would arrive later in the trip for a gig. Amato, who still is still friends with the band's former keyboardist,

Venier, soon found himself on stage with the band. Amato jammed with Venier and his bandmates before seeing Salvation play its late night set, which ended at 2 a.m.

When the bands stopped playing, the band members made their way to the third floor of the hotel where Cahoots resided. There they found the owner fast asleep in a sleeping bag.

Amato and Schraeger and members of the two other bands opened the bar and the musicians and their guests enjoyed free drinks for the remainder of the night.

One night later, the bands held a smaller, eight-person party inside Amato's hotel room. The drinks were flowing until about 6 a.m. when Lance Larson, an Asbury Park singer/guitarist announced, "We're all out of beer."

"Don't worry about it," Schraeger said.

Schraeger walked downstairs to the bar and snuck a case of Beck's back to the hotel room.

The escapades resumed and a woman Amato and Schraeger had met the previous night started pouring beer on herself. Amato became infuriated when the beer spilled onto his bed, so he and his musician friends chased her out of the room.

The woman fell asleep with the door to her room open, causing her puppy to run around in the hallway and soil the floor. When a barefoot Schraeger stepped in the shit and dragged the smell into Amato's room, the keyboardist reached his boiling point.

"What the fuck, this girl can't pick up her dog shit?" Amato said.

Amato picked up the shit with paper towels, wiped it on the side of the women's head, circled it with toothpaste and left her room.

Amato returned to his room where he found Schraeger and Larson still awake and restless for more action. The rest of their friends were

IN CAHOOTS, IN ASBURY PARK

sleeping. Amato and Larson, who lost track of time but estimated it was 4 a.m., seized the opportunity to dare Schraeger.

"I bet you don't have the balls to go outside naked," they told Schraeger.

Schraeger removed his clothes, put on LaBella's blue ski boots and headed out the door of the third floor ski lodge room.

After a few minutes Amato became suspicious, knowing that it didn't take very long to go down the steps. Amato peaked through the open door and noticed the tips of a pair of blue ski boots. Schraeger was trying to hide on the steps. Amato nudged Larson and tried to verbally coax Schraeger into completing the dare.

"Lance, when I get back to Asbury I'm going to tell everybody Schraeger is a pussy," Amato said.

After about two seconds, Amato heard the clanking of Schraeger's boots stomping onto the ground.

"Look at me, look at me," yelled the naked Schraeger, from the middle of the parking lot, as he jumped up and down in the snow.

Unbeknownst to all three participants who thought the parking lot was barren, the time was five hours later than they thought. It was really 9 a.m., the morning rush hour for families to start skiing. One station wagon, filled with a family on its way to ski, almost hit a telephone pole as the driver stared at the naked drummer.

If cell phones existed, Schraeger would have found himself in jail. Instead, it's a memory Schraeger and Amato still laugh about today.

During a separate occasion, Amato and Schraeger went to The Record Plant, in New York City, where Van Zandt was working on an E Street Band recording. While at the studio, Van Zandt asked them to help fix some issues his engineers were having with the drum sounds for "Darkness on the Edge of Town." During a break, Van Zandt pulled out a bottle of Courvoisier from the refrigerator. Amato and Van Zandt polished off the bottle, as Schraeger drank Miller High Life beer that he purchased for a quarter from the studio's vending machines.

Eventually, Amato and Schraeger left The Record Plant for their intended destination, Media Sound, a recording studio in the city. The band had not produced a satisfactory mix of a prior demo they recorded at Media Sound. Some of the band members tried to correct the mix, but weren't satisfied when they brought the demo home and listened to it. After Patti Scialfa, who worked at the studio, arranged a new mixing session, Amato brought Schraeger with him to the city to correct the mix.

After leaving The Record Plant, they decided to buy beer for the mixing session at Media Sound. Both in a drunken state, Amato and Schraeger left the liquor store and jumped into a cab on 38th Street with a brown paper bag filled with six packs of beer and headed towards the 70th block of New York City. The cab missed the studio and its driver let his passengers out at the top of a hill on 75th Street.

"Watch the beer," Amato said.

"I've got it," Schraeger replied.

The moisture of the cans caused the bag to rip open and sent the beer cans sputtering down the hill. Schraeger quickly chased after the cans and recovered about six. They headed to the upstairs of the studio's headquarters to salvage the fizzling beer and put the cans in the refrigerator.

Eventually, Amato went downstairs to mix the demo, while Schraeger continued to drink the beer alone upstairs. Time passed before Schraeger came down and said, "Ah, you've got to come upstairs, you'll never believe who is here. It's Frankie Valli."

"Oh, really?" Amato replied.

Amato walked upstairs, turned the corner of the studio's lobby and was acknowledged immediately by the legendary singer. Schraeger nearly

IN CAHOOTS, IN ASBURY PARK

had a cardiac arrest when he learned that the two men already knew each other.

"Hey Anthony, how are you doing?" said Valli, before he and his then wife, MaryAnn Hannigan walked over and hugged and kissed him.

"What the fuck is this? He knows him too?" Schraeger said.

Valli who was mixing "My Eyes Adored You," asked Amato to go into the studio room and listen to the freshly finished mix.

Schraeger called Van Zandt at The Record Plant.

"How the fuck does he know Frankie Valli?" Van Zandt said.

By that point in his career, Amato had already met many famous entertainers.

"You know these people after years of being in the business and they do hug you, because they respect you," Amato recalled.

Released by The Four Seasons in 1974, "My Eyes Adored You" reached number one of the Billboard Hot 100 chart.

Though the vast range of character traits in Cahoots sometimes caused friction, the band became a family.

"It was a very strange family," Oeser said. "We did hang onto it for quite a while. We probably outlasted most bands at the time."

Spending so much time together at home and on the road also spurred many fights. At one point, Oeser and his wife. Michael Scialfa and Schraeger rented a house together in Neptune. Oeser still remembered the empty 4-liter jugs of Pisano Wine that lined its floors.

Luraschi lived about a mile away and Amato resided near the Stone Pony. Oeser and Amato scuffled verbally on many occasions and other band members exchanged punches from time to time. Still, music was the common language that brought a sense of harmony to the band. The fights were never related to music.

"Once the music started, everything was great," Amato said. "Once the music stopped, mic stands went flying."

Alcohol was usually a factor. The easygoing Oeser, who rarely drank, remembered a drunk Schraeger plucking at his last nerve on one occasion. Oeser told Schraeger to shut his mouth more than once. Oeser turned to walk away, but like a dog repeatedly kicking a postman's heals, Schraeger continued his chatter.

"I am hoping that this only happened once (during the band's existence) but I definitely had him up off the floor by his neck," Oeser recalled. "It's the only one I remember and I'm not very fond of the thought."

Most of the band members were lucky enough to be standing out of harm's way as spectators at the other side of the bar, Amato said.

"It was really kind of hard to get John off of Steve because in reality, me, the other guys and Tommy LaBella were too busy cracking up," Amato said.

The spit that emanated from Schraeger's mouth when he tried to talk while drunk always made him even harder to take, Amato said.

"Schraeger was like a little terrier that won't shut up and when he used to drink it was unbearable," Oeser said.

Many times, as soon as the music ended at the conclusion of a set, microphone stands went flying. Luraschi had a habit of hitting Schraeger with the head of his bass guitar, every time the drummer missed a beat.

"If you check the back of Steve's head, he's got a couple of holes in there," Amato said.

Amato recalled one night when Luraschi hit Schraeger so hard, his bass drum and cymbals flew off of the stage.

The band's members still enjoyed performing together and creating musically spontaneous moments.

"Even when we were pissed at each other, it was fun," Amato said.

"We would end up laughing, "Schraeger added.

IN CAHOOTS, IN ASBURY PARK

Oeser remembered a heated argument he had with the Shots' lead singer Donnie "Birdman" Bertelson for sucker punching Tony Pallagrosi, trumpet player for Southside Johnny & The Asbury Jukes.

"You've got a chance to explain yourself and apologize or we'll just go at it right now," Oeser told Bertelson.

The two men exchanged words, before Bertelson apologized.

Despite the infighting, a brotherly bond emerged in Cahoots. Schraeger, a diehard New York Yankees fan, always watched the team's games in the house. Originally a San Francisco Giants fan to bust his father's chops, Oeser joined Schraeger in rooting for the struggling Yankees.

Cahoots even shared holidays with its members' relatives. Schraeger's parents joined Amato and their son for a Thanksgiving dinner, at the house both bandmates shared in Neptune. Seated at the dinner table, the hosts and guests heard screaming and moaning after Mike Scialfa and his girlfriend, Maria, had left the table and headed upstairs to have sex.

"Boy was I mad," Schraeger said. "I said, you couldn't wait until my parents left, Mike?"

Theiss suffered his share of hazing. Before one of Cahoots' shows at The Pony, Theiss told his wife not to let out that it was his birthday. His wife told Oeser, who relayed the information via microphone to the audience during the show. It wasn't long before separate people handed drinks of different colors to Theiss.

"The ass that I was, I took each one and downed it and gave them the glass back," Theiss recalled.

Unable to play, Theiss wound up sitting on the drum riser until he eventually left the stage.

"Steve Van Zandt came and finished the night out for me and I was in the back room laying on the couch," Theiss said. "Next thing I know, I open my eyes and there's Bruce and Steve standing over me, looking down and shaking their heads."

Cahoots' band members developed lifelong bonds after many experiences together. Theiss, who still lived in Freehold in the late 1970s, slept at LaBella's house many nights after gigs. Sitting on the front porch until about 5 a.m., LaBella would play his saxophone and the pair of bandmates would talk and observe their surroundings.

LaBella has always been straight forward and honest, Theiss said.

"We ended up pretty close," Theiss said.

Theiss said he has a great amount of trust for all of Cahoots' members.

Theiss also crashed at Amato's 4th Avenue home on many occasions.

"There was one night when I was sleeping on his couch and, that son of a bitch, I woke up with my finger in a bowl of water and him standing there waiting for me to piss my pants," recalled a laughing Theiss.

Chapter 20
The Split

"What the fuck do you mean, you're out of the band?"

In 1978, Cahoots' success resulted in a proposed record deal with Columbia Records, which ultimately caused friction between Theiss and his bandmates. Handling business for the band, under the guidance and mentorship of Van Zandt, Amato secured the band's first recording contract with a local manager. Before heading out to the Stone Pony for the night, Amato left the contract on the kitchen table at the house of a woman Springsteen was dating. Amato returned to the residence, where Springsteen screamed at him for signing a contract that was full of issues. Springsteen took Amato and Theiss to New York City, where

Josh Davidson

Springsteen's lawyers reviewed the contract and eventually had it nullified, Amato said.

One week later, at The Stone Pony, Springsteen frantically searched for Amato.

"I want the tapes," Amato recalled him saying.

Springsteen delivered Cahoots' recordings to Jon Landau, his manager at the time, and the band had the attention of Columbia Records. With The Shakes offered a deal by Epic Records, Bruce Springsteen and the E Street Band signed to Columbia and Southside Johnny and the Asbury Jukes already signed to Epic, Cahoots would potentially be the fourth.

As the band sought to take the next step towards its goal, Theiss wanted to decline the deal, Amato said. Amato recalled that Theiss immediately asked for a meeting at Springsteen's house, where he was met by Springsteen, Amato and LaBella. The meeting, described by Amato, took place when the record deal was only in the works and months before it was solidified. Cahoots was aware of a potential record deal, but a meeting with Columbia Records was not under discussion at the time.

According to Amato, Theiss told the individuals at the meeting that he enjoyed playing music, but didn't want to ride Springsteen's coattails to a fruitful career. Amato responded that Springsteen might get Cahoots through the door, but it would still be up to them to stay successful.

"It's up to you to stay there," Amato recalled telling Theiss. "It doesn't matter who gets you through the door."

Theiss still didn't understand that no band made it through the door of a record label without connections, Amato said.

"George's songs would have done very, very well, because there were a lot of similarities between George's and Bruce's work," Amato said.

IN CAHOOTS, IN ASBURY PARK

"They were different songs and had a different feel, but George on his own would have been great."

Theiss continued to argue against signing the deal, but finally agreed to proceed.

A few weeks later, Amato received a call from Mickey Eisner, of Columbia Records, who told him he would attend Cahoots' Stone Pony performance on the next Friday night where Cahoots would sign the contract. Springsteen would provide a lawyer to the band, Amato was told.

On Wednesday, elated over the news that a deal was in place, the band played exceptionally well at The Royal Manor, in Wall, N.J. Amato said.

Amato recounted the call he received from Theiss the next morning:

"I'm out of the band," Amato recalled Theiss telling him.

"What the fuck do you mean, you're out of the band?" Amato said.

"Well, I'm in Florida," Theiss said.

"How the fuck are you in Florida? You know we've got a gig Friday night at the Pony," Amato said.

"Well, I'm out of the band, I ain't making it," Theiss said.

"Do you know they're signing us?" Amato said.

"Well, I don't want it, we're too immature," Theiss said.

"Too immature? No fucking shit, we're 23 years old, of course we're immature — you fool," Amato said.

The call marked the end of Theiss' tenure with Cahoots.

"He threw the deal out the window," Amato said. "If you want to make a record deal, you get it when you are in your early 20s."

In response to Amato's account of the situation, Theiss said that he didn't think the record deal was in its final stages.

"I am not sure how real the record deal was," Theiss said. "I don't think the actual deal was in place and ready to go."

Theiss said he thought the record deal was more of a thought and not an actual record deal, which was ready for signature.

"It wasn't me saying no," he said. "It just wasn't there. It wasn't for real. It wasn't a positive deal. It wasn't, 'OK, we want you guys to come in and sign the deal.' We weren't at that stage."

However, Theiss acknowledged Amato had more insight into what was taking place than he did.

"I didn't know 100 percent what was going on," he said. "It was mostly my fault, but I don't think the deal was really in place. There wasn't a deal to be signed and ready to go. It wasn't me just saying, 'no, we're not going to do it.' They could have done it and I could have left the band. If I had said, 'no,' they could have replaced me."

Upon hearing of its potential deal with Columbia Records, Cahoots continued to focus on its music without letting excitement cloud its path. Detailed conversations with many label representatives gave Amato no time to bask in the moment. The band considered the deal to be an opportunity to work more and increase their fan base rather than a stamp of approval that made them better than other Asbury Park bands.

"We didn't see it coming, it just came," Amato said.

Amato's joy came with some skepticism since he knew that record deals had fallen through for some of his counterparts. However, Springsteen's backing of the deal made the latter highly unlikely.

"Bruce ain't going to bullshit you," Amato said. "Either you've got it or you don't. He'll tell you where it's at."

At the time, record companies supported bands better than they do today and gave them publishing deals at an even split, Amato said. Many of today's bands sign record deals, only to have their albums forever placed on the backburner.

IN CAHOOTS, IN ASBURY PARK

"You were getting a pretty decent deal from them," Amato said. "You did pretty well back then in the 70s with a record deal. You can't beat it. They would promote you and they would get you out there. And there was a guarantee that they weren't going to shelve you."

Other Asbury Park bands, including The Shakes, received and declined major label offers. Cleveland International offered The Shakes a deal in the late 1970s. The independent label eventually became a subsidiary of Epic Records. Shortly after Steve Popovich formed the label in 1977, it released Meat Loaf's "Bat Out of Hell" album, which eventually sold more than 40 million units. Popovich was instrumental in launching the careers of Southside Johnny & The Asbury Jukes, Boston and Cheap Trick.

Record companies simply did not offer more than an even split of publishing profits to emerging bands, Amato said.

"Even Bruce didn't have that until he got big," Amato said.

Theiss' bandmates saw red when the deal with Columbia Records fell through. The band had spent countless hours making Theiss' songs into their own. Springsteen and Van Zandt had already pulled many strings, but the deal was over, Amato said.

"He was better to go to Florida, because if he was in Jersey I would have been on his doorstep with a baseball bat," Amato said. "I felt like getting on a fucking plane. I wanted to go kill the son of a bitch. The whole band was screaming. The whole band was like, 'Is he out of his mind?' He's nuts. Get me a car. I'm going to find this fucker in Florida. I'm gonna break his legs."

Astonishment swelled across the Cahoots camp, as its management and sound team struggled to grasp Theiss' decision.

"Everybody is breaking their back and you turn and walk away," Amato said. "That's a hard thing to take."

After three decades had passed, the band members still remembered the potential deal. Springsteen got Cahoots' foot through the door of Columbia Records, but Amato's business expertise made the deal a viable possibility, Schraeger said.

"I never really talked to George about it," Schraeger said. "I have nothing against him. I don't know what the insecurity was about, if he was insecure of himself or us. But it would have been a much greater learning experience."

"It would have changed things," Oeser said.

Even if Theiss threw away everything the band had strived to achieve, Luraschi never blamed him for leaving.

"He had two kids to raise and I understand all of that," Luraschi said. "I was married at the time myself, but I had a very supportive wife."

Luraschi said he and Theiss remained very dear friends throughout their lives.

The toughest part for Amato was calling Springsteen, who placed his faith in the band and put the deal in place. Amato had to cancel two shows that were booked beforehand. However, shortly after Theiss left, Cahoots added Larson on rhythm guitar and vocals and DeSarno, formerly of The Shakes, on lead guitar and tried to move forward. The band broke up after playing a few gigs during a couple of months. Its members realized things weren't the same. Amato formed a new band, which consisted of frontman John Oeser, as well as Michael Scialfa, Luraschi, Larson, DeSarno and a horn section that included Tony Pallagrosi, LaBella and Pete Mauer. Amato left the new band before its name became Cold Blast and Steel II.

During the summer, Cold Blast and Steel II spent a lot of time traveling back and forth from Asbury Park, where it played at The Stone Pony, to the resort town of Wildwood, New Jersey, where it played at Art Stock's Playpen South, racking up five nightly gigs per week between both venues. The band also performed at many colleges on the East Coast. Though the group borrowed its name from the original Cold, Blast and Steel, it was not considered a spinoff. The band had more a rhythm and blues flavor than the original, which played straight ahead rock by artists such as ZZ Top.

"That band did really, really well," Schraeger said. "This was a band where we rehearsed every day. When we weren't playing a gig, we were rehearsing."

The group disbanded after about nine months, after Larson and DeSarno left to form The Lord Gunner Group. At the onset of the 1980s, Oeser took what would become a hiatus from the music industry to pursue other professions.

In 1979, Theiss called and asked Amato to join the George Theiss Band. Both men were ready to put the past behind them.

"The urge of killing him went away," Amato said.

The musicians of Asbury Park considered one another members of a family. Band members fought and reconciled on many occasions.

"How long are you going to stay mad at your brother?" Amato said. "You can't stay mad at your brother forever."

Chapter 21
The George Theiss Band

"I don't think anything is going to compare to Cahoots."- Theiss

In 1979, Amato joined Theiss, bassist Vinnie Roslin and drummer Eliott Bauer in The George Theiss Band. As the band's main singer, Theiss was exposed firsthand to the vocal stress test Oeser experienced with Cahoots. During the late 1970s, Cahoots blew through three-song Stevie Wonder medleys without pausing.

"Can you lower the key?" Oeser would ask.

"Yeah, we lowered it," his bandmates would respond.

"We never did, because it sounded better playing it where we were," Theiss said. "Vocally, it just tore him up."

Aside from performing Theiss' originals, The George Theiss Band covered various styles of music including songs by Van Morrison, Joe Walsh, The Rascals and many of Motown's classics. Theiss was mainly the lead singer, but other band members occasionally sang lead.

IN CAHOOTS, IN ASBURY PARK

The George Theiss Band, from left to right, Amato, Theiss, Bauer and Roslin.

Both Cahoots and The George Theiss Band produced some magical moments on stage where the music jelled dynamically, Theiss said.

"There were some nights when we were really on," he said. "It's when you're doing a specific part of a song that's building and building and building and you're really concerned, like, I know I'm going to forget the fucking note or somebody's going to screw up."

But everything would click and the result was magical, he said.

Aside from playing at The Stone Pony, The George Thiess Band played at Crazy Horse, a club in New Rochelle, New York which was owned by Vincent Pastore, who starred along with Van Zandt as the mobster Salvatore "Big Pussy" Bonpensiero on the HBO smash hit series "The Sopranos." The band would start late and play until the early morning. The band crashed at Pastore's house on many occasions before driving home the next morning. The band also played at venues such as the Capital Theater in Passaic, New Jersey, and Big Man's West, a club in Red Bank which was owned by Clemons.

The band enjoyed being able to leave everything on stage for an hour and half at The Stone Pony, where it opened for artists such as Edgar Winter and Mitch Ryder. Many times, Theiss got pissed after being asked to set up in front of the headliner's drum set.

"I would say fuck it, let's go out and tear it up," Theiss said. "So we went out there and we would tear it up as much as we could and we had a lot of good shows."

Theiss said he enjoyed playing at Mrs. Jay's with the George Theiss Band in the mid-1980s. He got to know and form good friendships with Eileen Chapman, who ran the club, and other members of the staff. Though the club didn't stock Grand Mariner, Chapman always ensured there was a bottle of the orange-flavored cognac liqueur reserved for Theiss.

"They are just good people," Theiss said. "We got along very well and that just held on for a very long time."

On one night, Theiss invited Springsteen to a George Theiss Band practice at the home of a bandmate's mother. He previously told Springsteen that he didn't want him coming on stage, because every time his band or The Jukes performed, the crowd would look for Springsteen. It wasn't as if Theiss was angry at Springsteen. He just wanted the crowd to experience the band without The Boss' presence.

"It does beef up your crowd, but I didn't want them coming to see him," Theiss said. "I wanted them to come and see us."

Springsteen did not attend the show, but did show up at the band's practice.

"He straps on a guitar and, again this goes back to us butting heads, and starts playing one of my songs," Theiss said. "And I looked him dead in the face and said, that sounds like you. And now when I think about it I am going, yeah, because that's how he plays. I wanted him to play something different, take it out of his style, take it out of my style. He

IN CAHOOTS, IN ASBURY PARK

was in his style, so what more could he have done, so I was kind of stupid at that."

Theiss was never shy about speaking his mind to Springsteen. One night at Big Man's West, Theiss stood next Springsteen. As a performer who resembled Springsteen performed in front of a nearly empty crowd, Springsteen told his ex-bandmate: "I like him." Theiss looked at Springsteen and said, "He thinks he's you."

"That's our relationship," Theiss said. "I'm not going to bullshit him and kiss his butt. He's my friend for what it's worth."

Theiss, who hasn't seen Springsteen in a long time, prefers to separate Springsteen's rock star status from their friendship.

"I don't want it to be about him being the rock star," Theiss said. "If we're friends, we're friends. If we're not, OK we're not. But sometimes that rock star thing can't help but get in the way."

Eventually, the George Theiss Band's members played in other projects while occasionally getting together for gigs. Performances soon became less frequent and were limited to sporadic benefit shows. Since LaBella was a full-time musician and part of many bands when he performed with The George Thiess Band, the band arranged its music based on his availability.

As years progressed, Theiss began writing music considerably less. He tried to focus on fine-tuning his originals and revising their arrangements, until his bandmates grew tired of repurposing them.

"I wanted to learn and develop and do more," Theiss said.

Theiss said he grew as a songwriter during his tenure with The George Theiss Band. He received many rejection letters from record labels he pursued. Many of the letters said, "You sound too much like Bruce," according to Theiss, "You don't sound enough like Bruce" or "We're doing Journey now, can you sound like Journey?"

Josh Davidson

Recently, from his home studio, which had the capability to digitally construct musical patterns and beats, Theiss spent as much time as he wanted retooling his songs. He played all of the string and keyboard instruments on his own and experimented with drum and horn loops and samples. He will quickly add a drum or bass track to his melodies, using computer software, before the idea was sent spinning into the black hole where songs by artists who fail to capture them go. The jingling in the depths of Theiss' prolific mind has been composed and delivered to audiences for many years. Over the years, Theiss was influenced by Van Morrison, Eric Clapton and Jeff Beck.

Theiss wrote and recorded hard edge rock, blues and even reworked some of his past material. Theiss hadn't tried to sell his songs to other artists, but sent them to his friends for feedback as he mixes and masters them. He always was excited, after completing a song. Theiss never forgot the glory days.

"I don't think anything is going to compare to Cahoots," Theiss said. "That was just a whole different thing. It was all the guys together, our relationships and how we played together."

Chapter 22
The End of an Era

"I think they paid you in cocaine." – Billy Hector, musician, regarding JP Maloney's on Main Street

In 1977, The Shots took over the Tuesday, Thursday and Sunday headlining slot at The Stone Pony that was formerly held by The Jukes. The Shots' lead singer, Donnie Bertelson, was a nimble frontman who, according to Hector, could do all of the "James Brown" moves on stage. Standing on stage, the Shots' lead guitarist, Hector, would watch Bertelson dip down while throwing the mic up, pull the mic with the cable, spin around on the floor and the jump back and grab the microphone all in about a second.

"I thought we were going to be the Rolling fuckin' Stones, after I saw that," Hector said.

As animated as an enemy of Bugs Bunny, Bertelson, who is now deceased, engaged the audience and his bandmates, getting in the face of his Shots counterparts as they laid down a solo, Hector said.

"Donnie was a great performer. He had charisma," Hector said. "He was a great storyteller. You would meet him once and you were endeared to him."

The Shots in 1977 near the Long Branch pier. (From left to right) Donnie Bertelson (vocals), Mel Hood (saxophone), Jim Heady (drums), Steve Rava (bass), Carlo Novi (saxophone), Tony Pallagrosi (trumpet), Davis Nunez (piano) and Billy Hector (guitar). (Photo by Lewis Bloom)

Since Bertelson was well known throughout the surrounding town of Neptune, The Pony would be packed when The Shots played. The band played many Jersey Shore nightclubs, including those in Atlantic City. Other members included Carlo Novi on saxophone, Dave Nunez on

IN CAHOOTS, IN ASBURY PARK

piano, Michael McCabe on drums, Steve Rava on bass and Mel Taylor on saxophone.

The Shots continued the tradition of playing five sets per night, with 20-minute breaks. For about a month, the energetic, eight-piece blues, funk, rock and soul band played Sunday matinee shows from 2-8 p.m. at The Pony. The band would then return at 10 p.m. and play until 3 a.m. On many nights, rock cover bands such as Stir Crazy could also be found on the club's stage. Fans lined up at the bar for the 10 cent beer specials. Many plunked a dollar on the alcohol-covered bar and walked away with 10 beers, Hector said.

After The Shots came Whistler and The Wheels, which included Hector on guitar, Pallagrosi on trumpet, Luraschi on bass, Schraeger on drums, LaBella on saxophone and Paul Whistler as the band's frontman.

The horn-infused band covered blues music, along with rhythm and blues by Stax Records' artists, including songs by Otis Redding and Wilson Pickett. But horn bands only drew modest crowds at The Pony once Asbury Park appearances by The Jukes diminished.

"After the first few gigs everything would be great; there would be 100 some-odd people there," Hector said. "At the next gig, there would be crickets – the band and their girlfriends."

Whistler and The Wheels experienced some success, but also struggled to fill the club at times.

"It wasn't a cake walk," Hector said. "You really had to work hard to make that work."

Whistler and the Wheels played a major benefit that summer with The Jukes for the legendary soul singer Jackie Wilson, who had suffered a stroke at a casino in Cherry Hill, New Jersey.

"The Wheels won the day," Hector said. "We were very good that day."

The band played at Mrs. Jay's and the Fast Lane in front of much smaller crowds than their prior bands. An agent representation deal with then Fast Lane owner Phil D'Angelo which would have resulted in a multitude of additional gigs fell through, but Whistler and the Wheels continued to rehearse at the club each day.

"We were just listening to, playing and learning music," Hector said. "It was fantastic."

During rehearsals, Hector taught the band how to prepare for playing at even the lowest volume levels by removing the microphones from practices, Schraeger said.

"We played and sang at a real low level, so it didn't matter where we were playing or what sized PA we were using," Schraeger said. "It was great. I learned a lot from that. Dynamically you would get really tight. You don't have to play loud to be good. It is always a pleasure seeing and playing with Billy, because I learned lot from him."

The band's budget was very tight. To supplement their lost income, Schraeger, Luraschi and Hector worked as bouncers at the Fast Lane, throwing rowdy patrons out of their seats and bringing in equipment for bands like The Ramones.

"I was the poorest as I was in my entire life," Hector said. "Schraeger use to bring me money for hamburgers."

Hector had known Schraeger since his days in Cahoots. Before he moved to the shore, Hector met Amato at a Jukes show at the Bottom Line in New York City. He met Luraschi, who was in his early 20s, during a Monday night open jam at The Warehouse. The scenario was similar to an old Western movie where Hector was the new kid in town. Hector signed up and walked on stage, where he met Luraschi, guitarist Stan Steele and drummer Mike Molinari for the first time. Steele looked and played like Peter Frampton at the time. The jam session that ensued

IN CAHOOTS, IN ASBURY PARK

more closely resembled a showdown between gunslingers of the Wild West.

"He was pretty pugnacious," Hector said of Luraschi. "So I picked up the guitar to play and he started yelling at me to get the hum out of the amp. So I said, it's not my amp, and then he says to me, 'You better not be a turkey on that guitar.'"

Hector called for the band to play the song "Situations" by Jeff Beck, since most musicians were familiar with the track.

"You'd better not be a turkey on that song," Luraschi warned.

Hector managed to hold his own on stage, though his style differed from the other musicians who surrounded him.

"We didn't leave the stage friends," Hector said of Luraschi.

As time went on and Hector played with The Shots, Luraschi came to respect Hector.

When Hector lived in Deal, which bordered northern Asbury Park, Luraschi worked in the antique store underneath the building where Hector lived. Hector visited the store on many occasions and the two musicians would talk and form a friendship. Luraschi and Pallagrosi were "ambassadors to the scene" who knew all of the right people. Pallagrosi asked Hector to come to Asbury Park in the first place.

Luraschi and Hector formed a close bond in Whistler and The Wheels. After leaving The Wheels in 1981, Hector, Schraeger and Luraschi formed Hot Romance with Don Erdman on vocals. The band added blues to its rhythm and blues repertoire and eventually released a vinyl record.

"We were trying to keep ourselves alive by doing covers, but continued doing originals," Hector said.

Blues was not popular during those years and even bands like The Allman Brothers Band were struggling to get work, he said.

"The blues was just not in," he said.

Josh Davidson

When Erdman was unavailable to sing on one night, Hot Romance tried squeezing in some blues rock by Cream.

"The crowd just emptied out. It was like magic," Hector said.

Hot Romance's originals received radio air play in New York City. By the early 1980s, Springsteen rehearsed with Cats on a Smooth Surface and made regular Stone Pony appearances with the band. Cats on a Smooth Surface performed at The Pony every Sunday night from 1979 through the early 1990s, O'Neill said.

"Holy shit, that was a great band," he said.

Hot Romance played to the overflow crowd at Mrs. Jays' biker bar. After its lead singer departed, Hot Romance asked Jon Bon Jovi to replace him.

"Obviously, he had other plans," Hector said.

Hector's spine-tickling picking over the Hot Romance's raw, original rock songs and covers by artists like Joe Jackson and Tom Petty created quite the buzz in Asbury Park and made Hot Romance a profitable venture.

Erdman eventually left the band to pursue a teaching career. He was replaced by Rick Fink, who now is the lead singer of the Gas House Gorillas. Soon after, the times became too hard to handle and the band broke up.

"After that I said, fuck it, I'll play the blues," Hector said. "Since nobody gives a shit, I don't give a shit."

So, Hector formed a blues band with Big Danny Gallagher and Vini "Mad Dog" Lopez on drums. The band played at some frightening Asbury Park joints like JP Maloney's on Main Street, a rough and tumble biker bar which was run by a nuclear physicist.

"If you didn't know anybody in there, you wouldn't want to go in," Hector said. "I just knew people, so it wasn't a stretch. It was dingy."

IN CAHOOTS, IN ASBURY PARK

Aside from regular gigs, Hector met many other musicians through jam sessions at the bar.

"I think they paid you in cocaine," he said.

Without the Internet as a resource to find other collaborators, musicians crawled clubs to find potential band mates.

"The bars were social media for musicians," Hector said. "It was where things would happen."

Some musicians like Gallagher, who lived above JP Maloney's, fit right in to the wild bars, but others didn't, like current E Street Band saxophonist Ed Manion, who a had straighter personality, Hector said.

In the mid-1980s, Gallagher, Hector, Manion and a harmonica player performed together in David Myers' Renegade Blues Band. Myers had been the bassist for the Blackberry Booze Band, which spurred into The Jukes.

"Sometimes they paid us in drinks, but when they found out how much Big Danny could drink, they stopped that," Hector said.

Hector remembered Gallagher, who he met through Luraschi, as a pleasant and jolly person.

"He was a great storyteller," Hector said.

Gallagher played a lap steel guitar while seated on a stool. During performances, he rose to his feet and sang songs like "Love Gravy," a crowd favorite, which he composed. Like Springsteen, Gallagher used his songs as a canvas to illustrate his experiences in the city.

Many times, he helped Hector move equipment in his big, red van.

"He was just like a big, Irish Santa Claus," Hector said. "'Big Danny' was all right."

Hector then founded The Fairlanes, a five-piece blues band, which released three albums on an independent record label. His new band played venues that included Country By the Sea, in Long Branch, whose large main room resembled The Stone Pony. On the side was a tiny room, with a small Go-Go Bar. The band played on Thursdays to about 20 people, but made some money while learning and playing the blues.

As it performed during the era prior to Stevie Ray Vaughn, the band struggled for audience interest.

"No one paid attention to what we were doing," Hector said.

In the late 1980s, bands became projects and musicians became "hired guns." The Fairlanes grew a following after adding dance music to its mostly blues repertoire, but Hector was challenged to find fill-ins for bandmates who had other gigs. The band consisted of Hector on lead guitar and vocals, Billy Lilly on harmonica and vocals, Tim Tindall on bass and "Boom" Carter drums. Hector's wife Suzan Lastovica sang, as well.

"She was the only woman at the bar a lot of times," Hector said.

One day, after consistently finding fill-ins for Tindall and Carter, Hector spoke with Richie "La Bamba" Rosenberg who faced the same challenge as his band, La Bamba and the Hub Caps, packed Asbury's clubs. Hector asked Rosenberg about his band.

"You mean, how are the 'Sub Caps?'" Rosenberg replied.

By 1988, Tindall supplied some of his own fill-ins on bass. Hector continued to network with other musicians and discovered a whole world of players who sought steady work. He overnighted Fairlanes recordings to potential fill-ins who would usually arrive unprepared to gigs. He sometimes enlisted Lastovica as a bassist when he couldn't find reliable musicians. The game of musical chairs became the norm.

"It took me years to get over that disappointment and now I live with it every day," Hector said.

In the early 1980s, Hector played every Sunday at Mrs. Jay's with Hot Romance. During the middle of the decade, he filled the same slot with The Fairlanes.

IN CAHOOTS, IN ASBURY PARK

As Mr. Jay's manager, Chapman reviewed The Pony's schedule and examined the type of music the club presented. When rock bands performed at The Pony, Chapman hired blues acts for Mrs. Jay's. If The Pony hosted a cover band, Mrs. Jay's brought in an original band. Rather than forging a competition, she intended to expand the area's level of variety by complementing the other clubs with separate musical offerings. The Pony had a solid mixture of original and cover bands. Cover bands like Backstreets, Sticky Fingers (which paid tribute to Springsteen and the Rolling Stones respectively) and Brian Kirk & The Jirks attracted crowds to The Jersey Shore. In the 1980s, Hitsville also brought big name acts to Ocean Avenue and Club Xanadu became a hotspot for disco fans.

"Clubs were coming and going, but there was always that variety," Chapman said.

Sharing a common wall where The Pony ended and Mrs. Jay's began, both clubs played host in the 1980s to the impromptu on-stage jam sessions that became an Asbury Park tradition in the preceding decades.

"After hours, the bands (from the Stone Pony) in the summer would come back to Mrs. Jay's and we would just sit in the beer garden all night, until the sun came up," Chapman said. "It was really a cool scene."

Mrs. Jay's was known for its local music and fine food, such as its huge "death" dogs and raw bar for visitors to the shore who craved shrimp and clams. Music on Sunday afternoons became an attraction for families and their children. The night drew mixed crowds of bikers, hippies and grandmas with their kids. Patrons sat at picnic tables, chatted with their families and old friends and met new people. The seasonal venue opened in April and closed by late September, Chapman said.

In the 1980s, the city was barren during the day, until music fans brought it to life in the evening. When Mrs. Jay's beer garden was an open area, the club's owners hired a security guard to occupy the club overnight in order to prevent theft from its beer taps.

"There were a couple of summers here where you could have stood in the middle of Ocean Avenue and not even worry about getting hit by a car," Chapman said. "You could probably have laid down in the middle of Ocean Avenue, because just nobody was here. But at night when those clubs opened, people came. That was the only reason people came for a while."

Rather than causing too much trouble in the 1980s, the bikers looked out for Mrs. Jay's, Chapman said. Some entered the parking lot with children in their sidecars and dogs by their sides. The bikers kept an eye on their motorcycles through the sliding glass doors in the front of the bar, as they drank pitchers of beer and hung out with their friends. When the bikers noticed suspicious activity in the bar, they reported it to management, Chapman said.

"It was almost like they wanted to ensure that they had a place to go to for the rest of their lives," she said.

The bikers also kept an eye out to ensure musicians, including Carter, were safe.

"When I played at Mrs. Jay's with The Fairlanes, I had protection," Carter said. "I had some friends who were bikers, who knew who I was and anytime I got a little bad look from one of the bikers or something, they would let him know who I was."

Suddenly, the gazing would cease.

One night, Carter was the only African-American present when he played at a party for a biker gang. A biker put his hand on Carter's shoulder.

"Don't worry about it, boy, we got your back, all these guys aren't gonna mess with you," the biker told Carter. "You just play your drums like you do."

IN CAHOOTS, IN ASBURY PARK

Carter obliged.

"They had my back," he said. "They were nice guys. As long as I played, I was good."

Carter did witness a number of fights in the bar, but for the most part the bikers' sole purpose was to have a good time. After one show, as Carter loaded his drums into his car that was parked in front of the bar, a drunk man started urinating on his wheels. Before Carter could walk over and talk to the man, Lilly pushed the man off of his car.

"Hey man, you know whose car this is?" Lilly told the man, before announcing it was Carter's.

"If you were in the band, everybody had your back," Carter said. "We were never alone."

During the 1980s, powdered drugs such as cocaine and the methamphetamine speed were used prevalently in Asbury Park. Cocaine use was also very rampant in New York City disco clubs, such as Studio 54, at 254 West 54th St. in Manhattan, which stayed in business from 1977-1981. Musicians could effortlessly obtain drugs in the New York City clubs, Carter said.

"I would sit down at my drums and there would be a line sitting on my drums," he said regarding some of his New York City gigs. "I would be like, 'where the hell did this come from?' You bend over and you do it. You snorted and, next thing you know, you are feeling fine, until the next time."

Disco began to re-emerge in Asbury Park and "cocaine was everywhere," Carter said.

"Everyone had that chemical thing going and, next you thing you know, everybody was running into each other," Carter said. "It got kind of out of hand."

The drug use yielded violent fights.

"It got violent, it got crazy, myself included," Carter said. "You get to a point where either you kick yourself in the butt and say, 'I have 'gotta' stop this' or you keep going and, next thing, you are dead or have nothing left. It was flowing like it was like snow all year long. It was so easy."

Crimes became more violent and the city began to decay, Carter said. Asbury Park's once safe streets, became very dangerous.

"Cocaine will force you to do things you would never think of doing," Carter said. "People were doing things that weren't them. And that's when you either stop or keep on going and you either go to jail, become really sick or die. You can't win."

Carter would go to sleep at 5 a.m. after a performance. Doing a line after waking up the next morning would enable him to play his next gig. When asked, Carter pondered if drugs negatively impacted his ability to perform.

"I would probably say no, but it probably did," he said. "If the whole band was doing it, then you would be like, we sound good. It was probably not the case. It was just too much. It takes too much out of you and takes too much out of your pocket. You lose a lot of things from it."

Drug use took its toll on many of the musicians Carter encountered.

"I hung out with people, I'm not mentioning names, that were in *Rolling Stone* magazine and they were doing lines with me," Carter said. "These were brilliant people. Everybody looks up to them and you would never know it. It was there."

Carter began to realize that he needed a change when he noticed that the balance in his bank account was nearly depleted and he couldn't pay his bills. He boarded a plane 28 years ago to start a new life in California and hasn't touched a drug since. Many of his friends from Asbury Park tell him they are scared to go near drugs.

IN CAHOOTS, IN ASBURY PARK

"I'm not ashamed to talk about it, because I know a lot of people did it and got hurt by it and a lot of people got out of it," he said. "I'm 62 and I can't even fathom even thinking about doing something like that."

Carter's departure from The Fairlanes marked the group's disbandment.

"Stevie Ray had already made it, so the blues had their hero and it didn't need another guitar God," Hector said.

Hector played with a number of drummers such as Van Romaine, who has played with the Dixie Dregs and Deep Purple, and Shawn Pelton of the Saturday Night Live Band. He still has a preferred affection for Carter's playing.

"Boom raised the bar of the drummers," Hector said.

Hector kept playing professionally, but had to turn to New York for musicians since most of Asbury Park's players gave up. He was one of the few musicians struggling to work four days per week, so he could pay his bills.

"I was doing it as a calling, as a living and a lot of the guys stopped," Hector said. "I was using the same gene pool that Southside Johnny was using for his players. The economics will make you pull away, if you're not really spiritually moved. If it is all about finance, you're in the wrong business."

He formed The Billy Hector Band in 1993 and experienced financial success two years later, as the economy surged. The commitment he made after Hot Romance broke up, to make a living as a musician, had paid off. The young musician was sitting naked, in a pool, with a beer and Marlboro cigarette, when he firmed up the decision. Erdman had just left the band after recording an album that took a year to pay off, but Hector decided to drive on as a professional musician. Most of Hector's memories, before and after that moment, were made on stage.

Hector was always enamored by artists like Hendrix who never failed to "expose the universe." Even on his worst night, Hendrix could "tear a hole into the cosmos and you would see globes spinning," Hector said.

"When that sound comes and it touches the audience, it moves every part of them," he said.

The bond between Asbury's musicians was similar to team sports, Hector said. Many conversed musically during improvised jam sessions. Together, they took a musical journey, lost consciousness and arrived home to the audience.

"Those were the holy shit moments," Hector said. "The scene is great, but the music is the real high. The music is where you pull back the fabric and look into the universe."

Hector still remains very active in the Jersey Shore music scene, playing 5-6 days per week. He recently released "The Fire Within," a four-song EP. He developed a trailer to promote the album, which is currently on YouTube. The release included the mainstays from his band, including Tindall on bass and current drummer Sim Cain, who has also played with the Rollins Band, as well as LaBella, and Bobby Bandiera, the current Bon Jovi guitarist, who has also performed with The Jukes and Cats on a Smooth Surface. The EP has a psychedelic sound with an eclectic mix of instruments such as violin, a harpsichord and mid-1960s sounding horns.

The release was recorded at Jankland Recording Studios with the help of Steve Jankowski who is the musical director for Blood, Sweat and Tears and Chicago.

"He has been a pro his whole life and he is just an amazing player and recording guy," Hector said.

Hector subsequently returned to his blues roots via the CD "Old School Thang." Driving audiences to the blues is still tough, but he plans on making an effort to bring new listeners to it.

IN CAHOOTS, IN ASBURY PARK

"The blues river is deep and wide," he said. "You can do a lot of things with it. You can do everything from Hendrix to Zeppelin to Count Basie to rockabilly and/or Prince. It's a big river."

He hopes to catch the attention of listeners in their early 30s, so he will have a blues audience for years to come. The bikers and Vietnam Veterans who used to attend his shows tend to not visit the bars lately, he said.

These days, Hector will gauge his audience's interest before deciding on a song. He tends to exclude standards, such as "Mustang Sally," from his set list.

"People come out just to see the art, so I try to be as artsy and musical as I can," he said.

How music is delivered to its listeners is currently undergoing a transformation, so the record industry will inevitably need to reinvent itself, Hector said.

"[The radio DJ] 'Cousin Brucie' doesn't dictate your taste anymore," he said. "You search your own shit out. Your friends tell you what they like. You take it or leave it."

After recording the song "Born to Run," Carter and Sancious left The E Street Band and formed the jazz fusion band Tone, with bassist Gerald Carboy. The mostly instrumental band later included vocalists Patti Scialfa, Gayle Moran and Alex Ligertwood, the former lead vocalist for Santana. The band recorded five albums on a major label in seven years and toured the U.S. and Europe.

"It was the best band I had ever been in," Carter said.

The band played structured, well-rehearsed songs. Jam sessions were mostly reserved for rehearsal. An issue with the record label disestablished the band, so Carter joined blues singer/harmonic player Paul Butterfield's band. He has since performed and recorded with major artists including Todd Rundgren, Nick Gravenites, John Lee Hooker and Bonnie Raitt.

After playing jazz and fusion with Sancious, The Fairlanes helped Carter rediscover the blues. After he first attempted a shuffle rhythm with the band, Carter determined he would need to work to bring it to his standards. So, he and Lilly drank Jack Daniels whiskey while listening to Lilly's large stack of blues records.

"I listened to all of these drummers, trying to figure out what I had to regain," Carter said.

It wasn't long before Carter fell madly in love with the blues again. The Fairlanes put the drummer back in touch with his blues roots.

Carter played guitar and percussion with The Jukes. He traveled with the band on a nice tour bus and had plenty of fun, but realized that being a percussionist wasn't for him.

He eventually joined the Lord Gunner Group with DeSarno and Larson.

"We were wild," Carter said. "We did everything fast. We had a good time."

The band didn't get too much sleep.

"We would play at night, get up at 10 in the morning, go to the bar and talk about it," Carter said. "I had a lot of fun with them and Lance, he is crazy. He kept us laughing all of the time."

Carter's heart is still heavy for the west side of Asbury Park. The clubs where he honed his craft and learned from the masters were destroyed in the riots and have not been rebuilt.

"That's why I cry when I go down there every time," Carter said. "I look at it and I visualize how it was and it's not there."

Carter currently records in his home studio in California, where has recently performed with Danny Click & The Hell Yeahs. After performing with The Red Bank Rockers for many years, Carter worked

IN CAHOOTS, IN ASBURY PARK

with Clemons in California. He enjoys being with his wife, the weather and good life in the "Sunshine State." His children are all grown.

"If I can do that through music, then I am even happier," he said.

He and Hector reunite with The Fairlanes ever year.

"Each time, it gets better and better," Carter said.

More than 44 years after the riots destroyed so many dreams, Carter still hears the influence and knowledge he attained in Asbury Park's music in his own playing. He's still plays music and walks freely on the beach.

"The west side is always going to be with me," Carter said. "The thing that's mine too is the Atlantic Ocean, even though it's on the east side. I don't think I would go more than a day without going down there every day of the week."

In his late 20s and early 30s, Luraschi began to perform on 250 nights per year. But nothing ever came easy to him. He struggled to find the right mix of musicians, which led him to experience bad friendships and working through disappointing musical projects.

"It's not like you parachuted in there and started playing," he said. "You've got to get money to live."

Luraschi, who experienced numerous life-altering hardships after losing his both of his parents in his early 20s, found salvation in music. He very rarely thought about quitting what was so important to him. Whenever the thought crossed his mind, he was fortunate to have true, sincere friends who supported and loved him.

"All I have are my friends," he said. "They are like my family. I mean we fight like brothers, I mean, literally kick the shit out of each other sometimes, but we get over it."

He struggled with drugs and alcohol during his life, before he succumbed to lung cancer at 57 in 2009.

"I've gotten through it, I've paid my consequences and I'll come out a better person for it," Luraschi said.

Luraschi stressed that he never wanted to go back to that state of existence and was thankful for being alive to tell his story. He met many other musicians in Asbury Park who weren't as lucky. Beginning at The Upstage, he met and built alliances with many role models who helped him prevail when times were tough.

"They conduct themselves in a civil fashion, which I hope and pray every day that I can do," he said.

Luraschi still thought about ending his musical journey and doing something else.

"If I put this much energy into any other kind of a business, I could probably be a quadruple zillionaire, but we all love it," he said. "When it's good it's great. You get those bright moments once in a while that pop up that make it all worth it."

Luraschi lived in other states such as Texas, none of which compared to Asbury Park. He has always considered himself a New Jerseyean and said he would never consider trading his experiences in Asbury Park.

"Yes, it's been good," Luraschi said. "There have been a lot of bad times, but it has also been good lot of times. It has all been worth it."

After years of playing in successful bands, Schraeger noticed a sudden drop off in opportunities for Asbury Park's musicians.

"You played gigs, but it wasn't like the past," Schraeger said. "Things had changed."

He started working a day job and joined a band with Gallagher. After his father passed away, Schraeger rented out his house and briefly lived in Ireland. He then returned to Asbury Park and lived with Amato. Schraeger played with Amato in a few other bands before he joined their current band, Boccigalupe & the Badboys, in 2000. The band's line up also included Luraschi and Amato, before Oeser joined in 2010.

Chapter 23
Boccigalupe & the Badboys

"His voice was an instrument that demanded your attention." – Paul Nelson, musician, regarding Oeser's voice

During his first rehearsal as Bonds' keyboardist, the soul singer walked over to Amato's organ and noticed sheet music sitting on its stand. Bonds picked up the sheet music and sent it flying in the air.

"I don't want that shit man, play the motherfucking song," Amato recalled Bonds saying.

To this day, Amato tells his bandmates to leave their notes at home. Trying to exactly replicate music recorded by other musicians constrains the entire band, reducing it to something like a karaoke machine, Amato said.

"You've got to play with your heart and your soul," Amato said. "That's the way that we do it."

Josh Davidson

Amato was an 18-year-old member of Brothers and Sisters when he first met Bonds at the Roman Arch in Asbury Park, at which Bonds appeared after performing at the Royal Manor in Wall Township.

"He got there late and was raring to play some music," Amato said.

After watching Brothers and Sisters perform, the owners of Pistol Pete's in Long Branch decided to open their club for a jam session. Bonds and Amato sang, as other musicians provided the instrumentation, and began a conversation.

"Gary has got to be one of the funniest motherfuckers I know," Amato said. "The man is totally nuts."

Before he left, Bonds gave Amato some advice.

"While Gary was leaving, he turns around and says, 'Tony, don't sing harmony anymore,' and he started cracking up and he left," Amato said. "That was my first encounter meeting Gary Bonds."

The two musicians met again at Bonds' Stone Pony show, following the release of a dedication album he made with Springsteen and Van Zandt. Amato joined Bonds' band and played large night clubs throughout the East Coast.

"There was always a lot of fun and a lot of laughing when I worked with Gary," Amato said.

Though Bonds has his own style of playing music and performing, he still exudes the same vibe and charisma possessed by Asbury Park's performers, Amato said.

"Gary was more or less an adopted member of the Asbury Park music scene," Amato said.

Following his stint with the George Theiss band, Amato and Bonds began spending more time together and have remained friends and sometimes bandmates ever since. They hung out every time Bonds went to the Pony and Amato spent more than a year as his keyboardist. Amato then became the keyboardist for the Bee Gees, a disco group formed by

IN CAHOOTS, IN ASBURY PARK

Australian brothers Barry, Maurice and Robin Gibb that has sold more than 120 million albums worldwide. Amato landing the job with the Bee Gees owed in large part to his father's friend, who was the Bee Gees' as the band's accountant. Prior to joining, he was unaware that he would be the band's third keyboardist, assigned to replicate the album version of the band's string and horn lines on the keys. Amato toured the world with the Bee Gees, stopping at destinations such as Australia, Europe and Japan, but never recorded with the band.

"They were a lot of fun — very mellow and very relaxed," he recalled. "It was just a group of guys hanging out and playing."

Amato's next band, Clarence Clemons & The Red Bank Rockers, shared Bonds' "just play the song" attitude. Bands that rigidly follow sheet music eliminate the challenge of being a musician, Amato said. Exact replication of a song can prevent musicians from completely experiencing the joy of playing, fully expressing their emotions and allowing a song to grow, he said. Amato's next band was Shore Patrol, which featured singer JT Bowen, who previously sang with The Vibratones and The Red Bank Rockers.

Josh Davidson

In the top photo, Amato enjoys the moment with Boccigalupe & the Badboys in 2015 at The Stone Pony. The bottom photo shows Amato, right, Schraeger, left, and the rest of the band during a separate show. (Photos by Conni Freestone)

IN CAHOOTS, IN ASBURY PARK

In 1998, Amato's current band, Boccigalupe & the Badboys, began to form when Amato was producing and playing some keyboards on an original release by local musician Kevin Ward. April Smith, of Toms River, was singing lead, but the songs weren't at satisfactory level for the project's members. One day in the studio, Amato asked for the song lyrics, stepped into the sound booth and managed to impress those present with his first attempt at singing lead, since he was a teenager.

"All of the sudden I was the lead singer," he said. "I didn't know I could do that. I never tried."

Amato, who at the time was singing some background vocals, produced the band and sang lead on some of its other songs. The resulting project was a band called Ill Spent Youth, which played Atlantic City and the Jersey Shore opening for artists like former Jimi Hendrix drummer Buddy Miles and Philadelphia rocker Robert Hazard. The band eventually became Boccigalupe & The Badboys.

One of Boccigalupe & The Badboys' first performances was in the center of downtown Freehold Borough. After one of the band's sets, Amato joined the crowd in the street and noticed Springsteen walking towards him.

"So, what are we doing?" Amato recalled Springsteen saying.

"I don't know what you're doing, but I'm going to do another set in about a half an hour," Amato replied.

"What? You don't want me to play?" Springsteen asked.

"Yes, I do want you to play with me, but not right now," Amato said.

"Why?"

"Because you're like the kiss of death, when you start playing with me," Amato replied.

"People are coming to coming to see me, for me."

"That will not happen with you," Springsteen replied.

"Why?"

"Because, it can't happen with you," Amato recalled Springsteen saying, as he walked away laughing.

Amato interpreted Springsteen's comment to mean that fans feel it is routine for Springsteen to play with him, since they grew up together more than 30 years ago. They won't view a Springsteen performance with Amato as they do the same scenario with newer bands.

Amato recalled Terry Magovern, Springsteen's personal assistant and longtime friend who passed away in 2007, frequently saying, "Well, if you can't get Bruce Springsteen, get Boccigalupe."

Schraeger recalled a night at The Pony, during which Magovern told him that seeing Boccigalupe & The Badboys was just like seeing The E Street Band.

Schraeger eventually joined Boccigalupe & The Badboys on drums in 2000 before Amato decided to bring Luraschi in as the band's bassist. LaBella performed briefly with the band and Oeser sang and played percussion for about three years until he passed away of cholangiocarcinoma, a rare bile duct cancer, in 2013.

Just before Oeser died, Theiss e-mailed him a song he recorded in his home studio with a request for a critique.

"Like the production and love the guitar," Oeser responded.

IN CAHOOTS, IN ASBURY PARK

(from left to right) Amato, Scialfa, Schraeger and Oeser celebrate Oeser's 60th birthday at Oeser's home.
(Photo courtesy of Marsha Amato)

Aside from Amato, the band's current lineup includes Paul Nelson on lead guitar, Tim Moss on drums, Bruce Martinez on bass, Jeff Smith on trombone and vocals and Joe Cunningham on sax, flute and vocals.

When all of the drum lessons for sixth graders were filled, the 11-year-old Nelson turned to the guitar. Now, nearly 45 years later, the Ewing, New Jersey, native's passion for playing hasn't subsided, even slightly. After beginning to perform with bands in high school, he fronted a solo project, the Paul Nelson Band, in the 1990s. He eventually recorded a CD with the Texas Alligators, before meeting Stevie Ray Vaughan three weeks prior to his death and founding a tribute band in his honor.

Josh Davidson

Throughout his career, Nelson could be found juggling three to five musical projects during a given time and performing every weekend. The genres ranged from country to the heavy metal sounds of his Black Sabbath tribute band. His main influences include Led Zeppelin, Stevie Ray Vaughan, Steve Cropper and southern rock bands.

"Tony's at the top of my list and I'm very proud to be in that band," Nelson said. "All of my other bands know it. He's a fun guy to play with and a good teacher."

As a frontman of other bands, Nelson knows being a band leader has its challenges. Nelson said he is impressed by Amato's ability to smoothly handle band-related adversity.

"Sometimes, when it rains, it just drips right off," Nelson said. "Tony is a cool cat that way."

Nelson is drawn to Boccigalupe & The Badboys' camaraderie and appreciative of the friendship he now has with its Asbury Park veterans. Schraeger, Amato and Oeser have helped Nelson improve his guitar tone and vocal harmonization skills.

"I'm definitely a better musician for knowing these guys," he said. "Each one of them has taken the time and tried to help me get even better."

Nelson had only set foot inside The Stone Pony less than a handful of times, before joining Boccigalupe & The Badboys four years ago. Now, he is glad to be a part of the current Asbury Park rock n' roll scene, with a band whose members he credits for creating it.

"It was all about the live show," he said. "I think that's where it started and that's where it still is, especially with these guys. It's in their hearts and souls."

He also had the opportunity to record on the band's final album with Oeser, "Never Needed Anyone" (Atlantis Records). Oeser always wore a smile and had an eagerness to open up to strangers through music,

IN CAHOOTS, IN ASBURY PARK

Nelson said. The two bandmates became close during trips to Canada, where the band performed shortly before Oeser's death.

"John was larger than life; he was a really nice guy," Nelson said. "I totally looked up to him."

Oeser was a true professional and a naturally talented performer who paid close attention to the intricate details of making music as a band, Nelson said.

"His voice was an instrument that demanded your attention," Nelson said.

Amato, Schraeger and Oeser resurrected many of the songs, first composed by Theiss, on the Boccigalupe & the Badboys album "Never Needed Anyone." The album's versions of "Rudy Vallee," "Just You and Me," and "Dreaming," may have been slightly modified, but they were driven by a group of men who started playing together as young musicians.

"I enjoyed doing George's songs again," Schraeger said. "John Oeser, may he rest in peace, sang 'Just You and Me' better than it has ever been sung."

Boccigalupe & the Badboys is essentially an extension of Cahoots, Amato said.

"The spirt is alive in the band," he said. "I'm not running around naked as much anymore."

Schraeger and Amato can still school any band who is willing to learn with their stage presence and musical proficiency. During shows, Amato still hops on his B-3 and plays the keys backwards. To this day, he said he can't play the solo for "Mustang Sally" as effectively from the conventional position.

During the recording process, Amato utilizes today's technology to share entire songs with the rest of the band. Amato presents a completely composed and recorded version of his songs to the band, which uses the demo to develop their own instrumentation. Armed with a fresh set of ideas, the band will then record the album.

"When I record with all of this shit, I still record it like I am back in 1975," Amato said.

Amato uses software to convert the digital sound into analog. He does not compromise when it comes to his preference for avoiding the excessively clean sound digital technology brings.

"Real music isn't clean. Elevator music is clean," Amato said. "When you play rock n' roll, you want it to be analog. It's fatter and it has a warmer sound than digital."

The first thing Amato sought when he used digital technology was software to convert the sound into analog, which has a fuller sound. Amato has utilized the skills of Mike Tarsia, a Philadelphia-based sound engineer, to enhance the band's recordings. Tarsia, the Pro Tools whiz who has worked with artists such as David Bowie, George Benson and Pattie LaBelle, came to Amato's home one weekend and helped him record all of the Hammond B-3 parts. Amato sent the final "Never Needed Anyone" recordings to Tarsia for mixing and mastering, but told Amato that the recordings did not need any further work.

Recording music from a home studio is much less expensive and more relaxed than using a private studio, Amato said. Without a time limit, Schraeger said he can attempt extra takes on his drum tracks.

"When you're in the studio and you're rushing to record something, you're trying to think about the sound, but you're spending the other half of the time looking at the clock," Amato said.

Just like Cahoots, the band practices hard to refine the material in its repertoire and learn brand new songs. The band still has the same spirit, switching song arrangements, improvising and keeping its audience engaged. Before most shows, Amato throws a set list on the floor, but his bandmates know that it holds as much weight as a counterfeit check. It's

IN CAHOOTS, IN ASBURY PARK

safe for them to assume the song order and arrangements will change. Repetition is equally as boring for both the band and audience.

"You can't do the same set list every night, because the crowd is not the same," Amato said. "You have to be able to read the crowd and connect with the crowd. If you can't read and connect with the crowd, stay home."

Sometimes at rehearsals, a band member will make the terminal mistake of uttering the phrase "well, on the record."

The bandmate can expect to experience Amato's wrath.

"Like the record? The record's been done already. Put yourself into it. Forget what's on the record," Amato tells them. "The record is just a map or guideline."

The band works tirelessly to keep the melody and meaning of every song intact, while driving the rhythm and feel down a different road.

Other Asbury Park artists like Bruce Springsteen & The E Street Band and Southside Johnny & The Asbury Jukes take the same approach to covering music by other artists.

"That's the whole thing in the Asbury music scene," Amato said. "Play it your way. Make it yours."

When Cahoots began playing, club owners urged the band to play covers, but the band still managed to sneak in originals that were disguised as covers. The band also spins its originals in different directions, allowing them to grow into a separate entity.

During performances, Amato and Schraeger look intensely at one another for cues that they will take a song down a new road. They stress the importance of looking at one another to the rest of their bandmates.

When Springsteen joined Boccigalupe & The Badboys on stage just before his first tour after the death of Clemons, the band missed or couldn't interpret The Boss' cue to stop the song during "Tenth Avenue Freeze-Out." The show, which occurred on Feb. 25, 2012, at The Press

Josh Davidson

Room in Asbury Park, was a benefit in honor of the deceased Tinton Falls, New Jersey, resident Tony Strollo. Strollo was Amato's cousin-in-law and Springsteen's personal trainer and bodyguard.

"When we got to the part that said, 'When the Big Man joined the band,' Bruce brought his guitar down — that means stop," Amato said.

Schraeger had his eyes on Amato, so he didn't see the cue. The rest of the band had never played with The Boss, so they did not know his signals.

"I was the only one who stopped," Amato said. "There was a brief pause, but we continued on. The effect would have a greater impact if everybody was watching Bruce."

"If I would have known, I would have stopped the band, but I didn't catch it," Schraeger said.

When members of Cahoots joined a band like The Shakes on stage in the late 1970s, a musician called out a key and the other musicians on stage joined in, regardless of whether or not they actually knew the song. The lead singer was the ringleader or quarterback who led the rest of the band through the rock n' roll and soul standards of the era.

"If the hand came down you would stop, if the hand made a circle you would go," Amato said. "It was all about paying attention.

Since the club's capacity is about 200 people, Amato tried to avoid the news becoming viral. With social media non-existent in the 1970s, fans attended shows to party and see The Jukes, without knowing if other musicians might appear, he said.

The fact that the Stone Pony house bands of the late 1970s were so familiar with one another meant there would be no issues when an influx of the musicians jammed together on stage. The countless hours they spent together off stage translated into tight on stage performances.

IN CAHOOTS, IN ASBURY PARK

"If you want to develop a good band, get the people you grew up with," Amato said. "I would never jam with strange bands. Fuck that. I might fuck up. I would jam with all of my friends."

Asbury Park's musicians of the 1970s knew when the time was right to stop rehearsing a song and bring it to the stage, Amato said. The growth potential of a song is limited at rehearsal, so in order for it to evolve, a band needs to bring to an audience, Amato said.

During the Van Zandt penned "Forever," Amato cues the band to completely stop the song for about two minutes, during which he walks around the stage. There is no stop in the original version.

"I can go to the bar to get a drink and then go back into the song or we can segue into a different song," Amato said.

Budget constraints have hugely impacted local bands who need to cover member salaries, transportation of equipment, gas, tolls and other expenses. The eight-piece Boccigalupe & The Badboys sometimes struggles to find gigs that are lucrative enough to support the whole band.

"The economy has gotten so bad that it's hard for places," Amato said. "They want you, but they can't afford to pay what (the band) needs."

Despite the fiscal challenges in both nations, music fans in England tend to see shows more than those in the U.S. When strapped for cash in its schools, America tends to cut funds from its music departments first, Amato said. When money issues arise, U.S. bars tend to follow suit by replacing live bands with disc jockeys, he said.

Chapter 24
Bruce Stalkers

"This is who we are. You take it or leave it." – "Boccigalupe"

There is a badge of honor, worn by many musicians who associate themselves with the "Sounds of Asbury Park." Some strut across the stage of the legendary Stone Pony, spastically flailing their arms, gyrating their flabby hips and falsely reminiscing about Asbury Park's glory days. Others wait backstage during a Springsteen appearance at a local club, well exceeding the legal confines of a restraining order in hopes of sharing a breath with the Boss. Like "cock-blocking" pledges at a fraternity party, they clamor for Springsteen's attention, validation and the opportunity to glorify their association with him. To meet Springsteen once is to say they've known him a lifetime.

IN CAHOOTS, IN ASBURY PARK

Those musicians who have truly earned the badge are hesitant to brandish it. They know the term "Sounds of Asbury Park" really represents an energy, charisma and attitude developed in the 1970s, and one which can't be mimicked or reproduced. They come from a small inner circle of bands that existed in the city in the late 1970s: The Shakes, The Asbury Jukes, Cahoots, The E Street Band and The Shots. They can legitimately talk about playing the Stone Pony regularly and being offered a record deal in the late 1970s.

"That's what really made you the 'Sounds of Asbury Park'; that was the formula," Amato said. "I don't care what anybody on the planet tells you. That is the real deal. If your name wasn't in *Rolling Stone* magazine for being the 'Sounds of Asbury Park,' you're not."

There is no shortage of frauds that associate themselves with the special era in Asbury Park's history, flashing the credentials of being "there" as a guise to entice people to their shows. But those who were truly "there" don't need to hint that a "special guest" might appear later in the night. The proof is in their music.

Amato and Schraeger still laugh at the dozens of local bands who say they were part of Asbury Park's music scene of the late 1970s.

"Who are these people?" Schraeger said. "We didn't see them back then. We didn't see these people in The Stone Pony in the 70s. Some weren't in the scene and some weren't even born yet."

"I like the ones that aren't even old enough and are running around today saying, 'Oh we're the 'Sounds of Asbury Park,'" Amato said. "Get the hell out of here. You're from New York, what do you know?"

The groupies who fought for Springsteen's attention in his days as a bachelor have been replaced by male musicians who fight for the chance to stand next to him on stage. Afraid to make it on their own merit, the stalkers disguised as musicians, sell the prospect of the Boss gloriously walking through the door at one of their shows, with a guitar in hand and jumping on stage. Some even strategically align their Asbury Park gigs with Springsteen's touring schedule and only play its clubs during his off nights. Promoters hint of a Springsteen appearance to try and lure fans to their venues. It's a shortcut to success that doesn't sit right with those who truly paid their dues.

"It's a sickness," Schraeger said. "Every time I see this stuff, it gets me irritated."

"It's just appalling to me how these people and promoters bullshit," Amato said. "We made it because we didn't bullshit. I'm doing OK with Boccigalupe & the Badboys because we don't bullshit. This is who we are. You take it or leave it."

Bands of any era or background that have the talent, drive and commitment to be successful don't need to ride another musician's coattails to fill a venue. Those who use Springsteen's name as a notoriety ploy struggle to draw even handful of fans to their shows when he is not in town.

"Bruce is causing all of these problems, because he is so great," Amato said.

Schraeger and Amato don't understand why some musicians fabricate relationships with Springsteen to promote their bands.

"Why these people do this is what I'm trying to figure out. To make themselves important?" Amato said. "You don't need to be important. Be who you are and I'll like you better. You don't have to know Bruce Springsteen for me to like you. You don't have to know Bruce Springsteen to impress me. You're not going to impress me. We have been on double dates, so you're not going to impress me – sorry. And this was way before he was married. It's the way it was. The way of the world. These people use this man's name ludicrously."

In the 1970s, a local newspaper coined the phrase "Sounds of Asbury Park" to describe the musical surge in the city. However, some argue that

IN CAHOOTS, IN ASBURY PARK

bands were distinguished by their charisma, vibe and energy rather than any common sound.

Those musicians who impacted the scene in the 1970s were part of a small inner circle, Schraeger said. Success was not automatic for any of them. The select few who were offered or received record deals paid their dues by consistently rehearsing and playing shows.

Each Asbury Park band had its own distinct sound, but they shared the common skill of making audiences scream and shuffle their feet on any night.

"We didn't sound like The Jukes, we didn't sound like The E Street Band, we didn't sound like The Shakes and they didn't sound like us," Amato said. "But it was the whole way that we would play on stage."

Chapter 25
After the Storm

*"Turn down the lights,
make them soft and low.
Just you and me, no matter where you want
to go.
Can you hear me talking?
I've got you on my mind.
Can we stay together, one more night?"
– from the Theiss-penned song "Just You
and Me"*

By the late 1970s, both The Shakes and Cahoots broke up, bands produced less original music and cover bands dominated The Stone Pony's stage, as the venue became cash-driven. The Stone Pony booked bands, such as Baby Blue, which focused on the popular songs of the era. Since playing covers at the venue was a profitable endeavor, bands traveled there from faraway locations with full PA systems and staffs of roadies that could rival a national touring act.

The scene began a downward spiral in the early 1980s, when the drinking age returned to 21, after it was lowered to 18 about nine years earlier. With police cars stationed on the path home, many clubgoers ran a greater risk of being pulled over. Stricter driving while intoxicated laws and proactive steps to enforce them made the area's streets safer, but also became what Hector called the final nail in the coffin.

Host laws made bar owners legally liable for drunks who got hurt after drinking at their establishment, Hector said. When liability insurance increased from $1,500 to $15,000-$20,000 per year, many bars either closed or gave up their liquor licenses, he said. Fire insurance premiums also rose to a level that was unaffordable for bar owners. The Jersey Shore was no longer lucrative for those individuals who were once lucky enough to make a living in music.

"People weren't going out and the bars were a little less full, so there wasn't as much money to throw around at bands," Hector said. "It was really just the end of a golden era."

In 1980, Hector struggled to find gigs for Hot Romance, as many of bars in Asbury Park and throughout the Jersey Shore closed and sold their liquor licenses.

"You guys sound great, but we're becoming a restaurant next week," the bar owners told him. "We just can't keep it together."

Disco grew in popularity and clubs owners chose to hire disc jockeys rather than bands.

"Who would rather spend $800 on a band when they could spend $200 on a DJ?" Amato said.

The Asbury Park boardwalk in 1981. (Photo by Lewis Bloom)

Years of reported and alleged corruption and inactivity by its governing body caught up with the city. The urban blight that emerged and spread throughout the 1970s ultimately led to its demise in the 1980s.

"The only commerce that was going on in town were the bars, and as soon as the drinking age changed that ended that golden goose," Oeser said.

Much of the city's decline in the early 1980s was due to the opening of the Seaview Square Mall, near the Asbury circle off Route 35 in Ocean Township, said Chapman, today a member of Asbury Park's City Council. Many downtown businesses left and some opened stores in the new mall. A sprawling state psychiatric care campus in Marlboro Township, Freehold's neighbor to the north, began phasing out its operations and relocating many of its tenants to boarding houses in

IN CAHOOTS, IN ASBURY PARK

Asbury Park. Induced with heavy medication, many of them walked the city's streets during the day.

"I think there were so many contributing factors to Asbury's decline at that point," Chapman said.

For periods of time, as the 1980s progressed, the city would awake at night when crowds filled the clubs, though far more modestly than in the preceding decade. At one point in the 1980s, John Shear stopped hosting shows at Convention Hall and the boardwalk casino, which drew thousands of people to the city. Shortly after, concertgoers who would have attended those shows spilled into Asbury's clubs. But the spillover crowds eventually stopped coming to the city.

As the decade concluded and turned, The Stone Pony, Fast Lane, Mrs. Jay's and The Wonder Bar drew respectable crowds and T-Birds opened on Main Street. The styles of music in Asbury Park's clubs transformed to singer/songwriter-type roots and folk rock in T-Birds and punk rock in the Fast Lane.

"The music content was broader and I think the audiences became broader," Chapman said.

"These were people who didn't really care about what the city looked like. They were coming for the music scene."

Major labels continued to scout Asbury Park bands in the 1990s. Other bands which have played in the city have signed recording deals, including Outcry, Highway 9, Red House and Bruce Tunkel.

"Even into the 90s there was still some label interest," Chapman said. "Of course that industry has completely imploded, so you don't get those A&R guys out there anymore to scout bands. Asbury was always one of those places where people came to check out the music scene and the current bands."

In the 1990s, the Saint and T-Birds thrived a few blocks from the boardwalk. Since 1994, the Saint has been a hot spot for fans hoping to catch independent and mainstream artists in an intimate setting. The Saint has always been a stomping ground for local veteran musicians and a place for younger players to aspire to. Following a morning performance on "Live With Regis and Kathy Lee," Jewel headed to the Saint in the evening to play what would be her first New Jersey show.

 Though the club was afraid she wouldn't be able to perform due to an illness, the folk/rock singer/songwriter sat in her car until she felt better. An appearance of the Ben Folds Five is another that almost never occurred at the Saint. Prior to sound check, the band's truck broke down and it barely made it to the club. Scott Stamper originally opened the Saint with his friend Adam Weisberg, an attorney who had worked at T-Birds and The Fast Lane. Located on Main Street in Asbury Park, T-Birds once played host to Jeff Buckley. When T-Birds closed, the two opened the Saint through the Asbury Music Company at 601 Main St., the former location of O'Shea's Rock & Blues in Asbury Park. After it opened, the Saint continued T-Birds' theme of being purely original and hosting up-and-coming national and local bands.

 The city made substantial progress in the mid-2000s when a developer rehabilitated the boardwalk's pavilions and found tenants for them. The influx of top quality restaurants was the main factor that drew interest, Gilmour said. In 2002, Moonstruck Restaurant & Cocktail Lounge opened at the location of the former Deck House bar, at 517 Lake Ave., and pioneered the restaurant resurgence. It was a time when crime and other issues discouraged business in the city. The restaurant had a solid following at its prior location in an Ocean Grove store front. In order to obtain a liquor license, its owners moved to Asbury Park and spent $2 million converting the former bar into what was arguably the Jersey Shore's trendiest restaurant. The restaurant's success encouraged others to follow suit. Today, Asbury Park's reputation as a dining destination is a bonafide draw for tourists, Gilmour said.

IN CAHOOTS, IN ASBURY PARK

Today, Cookman Avenue is lined with businesses which bustle on weekends, even after the summer tourism season. Along the strip, Cookman Creamery offers "homemade quality ice cream" and The ShowRoom cinema runs art movies. Asbury Park visitors can shop for clothes, eat, purchase paintings, get a manicure or a three-day cleanse – all on the same block. Though the recent resurgence may not signify a renaissance, the progress is encouraging.

From the 1990s through today, original bands have rocked the shore with styles including modern rock, funk, jazz, blues and metal. The Stone Pony hosts popular national acts, while The Wonder Bar books local artists of the past and present. Though it is hard to pinpoint the impact music has contributed towards Asbury Park's revenue, it has re-established the city as a hot spot, Gilmour said. Doing so has helped improve real estate sales. Gilmour uses the music scene to recruit business owners, who he brings to the The Stone Pony, during trips to view commercial space. At the onset of the Great Recession, city officials used music to stimulate Asbury Park's economy, Gilmour said.

"Music is just a great economic engine, so we're just using that as much as we possibly can now to get people to come here and support the city," he said.

People from all over the world visit the city during any given week to experience its history or take a picture in front of its landmarks. Many international visitors will spend a few days in Asbury Park on their way to New York City.

"We get visitors from all over the world and of course a lot of that has to do with Bruce," Gilmour said. "He's just an international icon."

The city is currently working towards diminishing its dependence on the beach and seasonal commerce, Gilmour said.

"Most of our businesses on the beachfront right now stay open all year long, so we are really trying to establish ourselves as a great place to come in the summertime, but we also want people to know it's a great place to come in February too," Gilmour said.

Asbury Park is unique in New Jersey in that it is not a seaside town, but one of the few urban areas on the Atlantic Ocean. Residents move to Asbury Park seeking city life with access to the beach, Gilmour said.

Asbury Park is currently home to 18,000 people and an additional 20,000 people visit Asbury during the July 4th timeframe, Gilmour said. The number of visitors who come to enjoy the beach, boardwalk, restaurants and music can sometimes reach the 25,000 mark. During a three-day weekend in the summer of 2013, when Asbury Park hosted its Bamboozle Music Festival, about 90,000 people visited the city, he said.

"We're just really trying to promote all of the great music that happened in the city," Gilmour said. "The music scene is alive and very well here right now."

Impressed by the downtown of today, Hannan doesn't think the magic she experienced in the 1970s will reoccur, since sequels are never as good as the original. People will always compare the new version of the music scene to the 70s. Legal restrictions and logistical challenges may also prevent such a reoccurrence, Cambria said.

"There will be something new and different and probably totally fabulous," Hannan said. "There are talented young people who are amazing."

Theiss recently visited The Stone Pony to see his nephew's band perform. He still misses the days of walking through the front door without stopping at the ticket window, since all of the bouncers, owners and bartenders knew him. He has always felt comfortable playing at The Stone Pony. It was a place where Theiss and his bandmates were empowered to grow as musicians, with little input on what to play.

IN CAHOOTS, IN ASBURY PARK

"It's like going to a house you used to live in and sitting in your bedroom going, man they fucking changed it," he said. "It looks the same, but it just doesn't have the same feel."

Matthews is encouraged by the recent signs of life within the city. Returning to the city still reminds him of the heyday, when he hung out with hippies on its board walk in the 1970s and listened to rhythm and blues and folk rock in its clubs in the 1980s. Though many of the bars and structures have been closed or demolished, there is still enough history to trigger memories.

"I was down there for the 4th of July the last couple of years and it kind of brought back memories," he said. "It wasn't the same, but there was life at least. The boardwalk is just a special place."

It didn't take long for the resilient city to revive itself following Hurricane Sandy, which caused $65 billion of damage in the U.S. in October 2012. The storm destroyed about 66,000 square-feet of the city's boardwalk and literally blew into boardwalk businesses, such as Langosta Lounge and The Silver Pinball Museum, causing enough damage to keep the businesses closed for months.

The Stone Pony was constructed far away enough from the shoreline to avoid major damage and The Wonder Bar was unharmed. Asbury Park's residents and business owners helped the city recover quickly and went to work shortly after in support of efforts to resurrect other local municipalities. Across the Jersey Shore, Hurricane Sandy destroyed hundreds of homes and businesses in towns such as Belmar, Mantoloking, Seaside Park and Seaside Heights. Boardwalks were demolished in many places and most of the amusement rides were wiped out in both Seaside Park and Seaside Heights, where artists such as Cahoots, Pallagrosi and Hector had once performed.

On Feb. 16, 2013, Amato visited Art Alexakis, vocalist and guitarist of the band Everclear, at Jenkinson's Night Club. Everclear headlined a show with Brian Kirk & the Jirks, which re-opened the damaged club and raised money in support of victims of the storm. For many years, thousands of young Jersey Shore cover band fans have packed the club for performances by the Nerds, the Benjamins, Dog Voices and Big Orange Cone. By destroying so many East Coast clubs, Hurricane Sandy forced bands such as the Benjamins into a scramble to fill some potentially profitable, but cancelled gigs.

"We had some big nights we had to reschedule because of the damage to the places we play," said Jeremy Mykietyn, the band's drummer. "We had to find a new spot for Thanksgiving Eve and New Year's Eve. It was rough. I think New Jersey was resilient because of the love for the area. Everyone has a great memory of their time here, whether as a child or grown up. And that sentiment fueled the recovery. Some areas have been slow to come back, but this year (2014) has been better than last."

The North Jersey band calls the Jersey Shore its home away from home. The band has performed covers throughout the East Coast at locations including Seaside Heights, Point Pleasant and Long Beach Island (LBI). New Jersey audiences are unique in that they include a wide variety of people, from many locations, who concentrate themselves in small sections of the state for entertainment.

"We have been able to perform professionally for nearly 15 years, in part to the reputation we have built from performing at the shore," Mykietyn said. "Now, we are doing more weddings, and it seems like every other couple has a special attachment to the band from seeing us in LBI or Point Beach. The energy from the Shore is magical. There's a feeling you can't get anywhere else performing at the Shore."

The band has written its share of original music over the years and plans to release new songs in 2015. Social media has been a game changer for the band's promotional effort. The Benjamins, which once used

IN CAHOOTS, IN ASBURY PARK

mailing lists, entertainment papers and word of mouth to garner a fan base, now relies on social media, Mykietyn said.

"It made things easier and more accessible, but it also created a lot of noise," he said. "People's attention spans have become so short. I think it's harder than ever to get people to pay attention (to bands' promotional efforts)."

Many years ago, when cement was poured in front of The Stone Pony, the club's cast of elite musicians carved their names into the sidewalk. But after returning to the club, following a recent renovation, Chapman no longer saw the names.

"They had taken up the sidewalk and put down a clean slate," Chapman said.

In 2002, when developer Asbury Partners considered demolishing The Stone Pony, Chapman joined the efforts to save the club. She talked to Asbury Park city officials about placing paving stones throughout the city to pay homage to the musicians who helped cement the club's reputation. She eventually ran into Pallagrosi at a Monmouth University concert and found out that their mutual friend, Novi, had passed away. Novi was in the process of developing a book, so he could pass along his musical roots on to his daughter. Chapman and Pallagrosi discussed her conversation with the city officials and determined they should develop a tribute for deceased Asbury Park musicians. She spoke with Jacqueline Pappas, executive director of the Asbury Park Chamber of Commerce, who was developing a project where members of the community could purchase name plaques on the boardwalk's benches. Chapman told Pappas that the three needed to discuss a plan to dedicate the benches to Asbury's deceased musicians. The project became known as "Asbury Angels."

"The three of us got together, put together a proposal, went to city hall with it and we got approval to do this," Chapman said.

The city is not funding the effort, but has granted approval to put the plaques on city benches and agreed to maintain them. The group formed an advisory committee, which researches a list of candidates and chooses 10 angels each year. Luraschi and Oeser are both Asbury Angels.

"It has been quite a journey with the Asbury Angels," Chapman said. "It's very emotional and the families are just amazing."

For the last three years, at least one family had a memorial service to coincide with the induction ceremony, where fans and friends pay tribute to the musicians.

(left to right) Schraeger, Amato, Scialfa, LaBella and Theiss during the Dec. 6, 2013 show at The Stone Pony.
(Photo by Conni Freestone)

"It's meant a lot," Chapman said. "We all wear sunglasses and cry as we're doing it. These are people who shouldn't be forgotten for any reason."

On Dec. 6, 2013, Cahoots' members reunited, as a band of brothers, using the language of music to express their deep, sincere love of a deceased comrade, Oeser, in their home, The Stone Pony. It was a house packed with smiling faces, memories and some of the best music that has

IN CAHOOTS, IN ASBURY PARK

bounced between the venue's walls. About one month prior, Oeser died of cancer at the age of 61.

Prior to the show, with a smile permanently pasted on his face, Theiss reviewed the songs with his brothers back stage. LaBella and the band's young horn section posed for band photos, as if they had been a unit for years. Whistler and Schraeger traded wise cracks, like it was 1978.

Oeser's white dress hat as his former band members prepared to pay tribute to him at The Stone Pony on Dec. 6, 2013.
(Photo by Conni Freestone)

As show time neared, Amato was all business. He walked on stage with Oeser's white dress hat in hand, carefully placing it on a mic stand in the singer's spot on stage. The crowd grew silent. The lights dimmed. A spotlight shined on the hat, as the Theiss penned "Just You and Me," serenaded the audience gently through the house speakers.

Eyes welled up and hearts were weak, as Oeser's family and friends could hear Oeser sing:
"Turn down the lights,
make them soft and low.
Just you and me, no matter where you want to go.

Josh Davidson

Can you hear me talking?
I've got you on my mind.
Can we stay together, one more night?"
As Boccigalupe & The Badboys' performance raved on, one could only wonder if somewhere in the universe, Luraschi was squeaking a ratchet, standing high on a ladder and stealing equipment to share with his brothers during their next journey. Or, was Oeser somewhere singing along to a vinyl record, trying to improve a voice that brought so many clubs to life? As every living member of Cahoots stood where they belonged that night, on stage at The Stone Pony, there were two empty spaces on the crowded stage, where Amato, Schraeger, Theiss, LaBella and Mike Scialfa were jamming in the presence of angels.

Chapter 26
Where the Bands Are: The Clubs of Asbury Park

"If you told your mother you were going to have a 'urine' card or 'good place to get a little' on your shirt, she would probably say, 'no, you can't go.'" - Hannan

Asbury Park's cast of characters stamped their signature on a historical rock n' roll era in a wide range of musical venues. Parallel and surrounding the boardwalk were an eclectic mix of clubs where many stories were to be made. Most Asbury Park bars of the mid-1970s were sparsely designed, with only a bar and stage between wood-coated walls. The reference section of *In Cahoots, In Asbury Park*, only scratches the surface of these clubs. Readers are strongly encouraged to visit and speak with the many musicians and fans that experienced the city and its venues firsthand. Undoubtedly, there are many more stories to tell.

Though this book already contains extensive coverage of The Stone Pony, its significance in the Asbury Park music scene warrants a second reference. A few years after opening as a disco club on Feb. 8, 1974, The Stone Pony became a place where rock n' rollers were handed "Urine" cards by its owners. Others bought t-shirts that referred to the venue as a "good place to get a little."

"If you told your mother you were going to have a 'urine' card or 'good place to get a little' on your shirt, she would probably say, 'no, you can't go,'" said Joy Hannan, who frequented the club in the late 1970s.

"So, we moved out," said Joan Cambria, her best friend.

By the late 1970s, The Pony was always packed. Crowds dwindled slightly in the winter, but the house bands continued to rock the stage.

"In the summer time, it was just wall-to wall," Hector said.

The rock n' rollers' style of dress at The Pony in the late 1970s consisted mostly of jeans and platform shoes, Cambria said. Women always wore pants and usually jeans. Denim clothing, "hip huggers" and most of the clothes worn today were in style, Hannan said.

"The disco fans dressed way differently than the rock n' rollers," Cambria said.

When the two former bouncers, John P. "Jack" Roig and Robert ""Butch" Pielka, first converted the front of **Mrs. Jay's** into The Stone Pony, the dress code did not permit jeans.

Until The Jukes produced enough revenue for The Pony, bands had to bring and set up their own sound systems. Many of the roadies who worked with these bands eventually went on to bigger venues in support of major artists like Bon Jovi and Bob Dylan.

IN CAHOOTS, IN ASBURY PARK

Today's outdoor concert area of The Stone Pony was once an outdoor, fenced beer garden, which was part of Mrs. Jays. In the 1970s, Mrs. Jay's offered cheap pitchers of beer, good food and quality local bands in the genres of folk, country and rock. Just next to Mrs. Jay's, at the corner of First and Kingsley Avenues, was the **Gold Digger** club, which featured lounge music.

Bars like Mrs. Jay's drew a contingent of bikers. On one night, The Stone Pony's owners and founders, Roig and Pielka, tried to eliminate the biker presence at a Cold, Blast and Steel show at The Stone Pony.

Schraeger recalled them telling the bikers before the show, "If you guys want to see this band, you can't wear your colors."

On the following Sunday, a slew of bikers pulled into The Stone Pony parking lot wearing button down dress shirts and ties, Schraeger said.

The Stone Pony's interior also contrasted from what exists today, in many ways. The merchandise booth, presently next to the main entrance, was filled with tables. A tabled section also filled up the area in front of the left side of the stage. Since it was in the process of making history, The Stone Pony also lacked the memorabilia that lines its walls today. In fact, the walls contained only sparse decorations, such as paper posters and flyers. The historical photos and signed musical instruments fans see today were non-existent on its bare walls, and large ropes hung from its ceiling.

Since it was about 75 percent smaller than it is today, The Stone Pony offered minimal space for sound fighting to travel between its walls. The club slowly grew larger as years progressed. Its earliest renovations occurred in 1975 with the addition of a raised seating and dining area, which still exists in the back of the club. The extended back room and bar that lie to the right of the stage today was a hallway that led to an office and bathrooms. At the end of the hall was a kitchen where

Josh Davidson

Springsteen and other musicians stored their gear, since the apartments they lived in provided minuscule storage space.

Many of The Pony's patrons frequented the **Quack, Quack**, formerly the **Empire Bar**, which was contiguous to The Pony. Without live music, the bar had a quieter ambience, so people went there to talk, Cambria said.

The Fast Lane first opened in 1974 as **Rocky's Warehouse Saloon**, before closing two years later. The club reopened as **Hotel California** in 1977 and became The Fast Lane in 1978. The Fast Lane hosted many national touring artists like The Ramones and U2, who rocked the club twice in 1981, early in the band's career. Other artists who have performed at the venue include fusion guitarist Allan Holdsworth, roots rocker Marshall Crenshaw and Jon Bon Jovi's early bands. As a high school senior, Bon Jovi played covers by artists like Springsteen and The Jukes at the club with his band Atlantic City Expressway, before doing so with The Wild Ones and The Rest.

Growing up in Sayreville, New Jersey, by the early 1980s, Bon Jovi's main aspiration was to be a Juke. His career, however, soared past the level of success attained by his idol, Southside Johnny Lyon. In 1983, his song "Runaway," featured on a local rock band compilation, received airplay on New York's former rock station WAPP. He put together a band of local musicians to play local shows and contests in support of the single. Three years later, Bon Jovi, Richie Sambora (guitar), Alec John Such (bass), Tico Torres (drums) and David Bryan (keyboardist) were bonafide rock stars.

In 1979, during a conversation following a Ramones performance at the Fast Lane, the band's singer, Joey Ramone, asked Springsteen to write a song for the punk rock group, which formed in Queens, New York in 1974. He did. The song, "Hungry Heart," was never recorded by the Ramones, but climbed all the way to number five on the Billboard

IN CAHOOTS, IN ASBURY PARK

Hot 100 chart, after it was released on Springsteen's 1980 album "The River" (Columbia Records).

The Fast Lane's interior resembled a large warehouse, with a tiny stage and an aesthetically pleasing bar. The bar was embedded with coins and many times covered with matchbooks, said Tom Matthews, an Asbury Park fan.

Patrons turned away at The Pony's doors eventually landed in other smaller bars like **The Wonder Bar** or **The Alamo**, Amato said. Some made their way to **The Student Prince**, knowing that Springsteen frequently played at the club. Before the night concluded, they would make a final attempt to enter The Pony.

Smaller venues like The Student Prince and The Alamo drew mostly students from **Monmouth College** (now University) in West Long Branch. Most of the students would start partying at the college before making their way to Asbury Park. The students headed back and forth between the city and the nearby college repeatedly during the same night. For many of them, a typical night ended with breakfast at the **Ink Well** coffee house in Long Branch beginning at 2:30 a.m. The Ink Well did not have live music, but remained open until 4 or 5 a.m.

"You would get done drinking and you would want to go eat," Amato said. "You would go to The Inkwell and have breakfast. That place was always packed and sometimes there was a line."

In the 1970s, Monmouth College's auditorium hosted local and national bands. Shows didn't occur as frequently as **Convention Hall**, but the college did provide a place for fans like Schraeger to see the hottest musical acts, including B.B. King, England's Climax Blues Band and Jethro Tull. During many performances, Cahoots filled the college's auditorium with young students who would make their way to the Stone Pony afterwards.

A wide variety of on-campus activities spilled into Asbury Park. After training sessions at the college during the 1970s, members of the New York Knicks meandered over to The Pony to catch Cahoots' shows. Throughout the 1970s, the city still offered classy movie theaters, carnival games, a non-gambling casino and a variety of musical genres to visitors and residents.

"There were 21 bars on that whole strip at one point," Amato said. "There was a total mix of all kinds of music."

The Student Prince was located at 911 Kingsley Ave., in a building contiguous to a Chinese restaurant. In close proximity with The Stone Pony and former Sunshine Inn, the two buildings now house a club and the Porta Italian restaurant, where patrons eat dishes like steak pizzaiola and seafood minestrone or enjoy drinks at the bar. But before becoming Porta and housing other businesses, The Student Prince became The Drift Inn, a tiny go-go bar.

With a maximum capacity of about 100 people, The Student Prince hosted many Monmouth County-based blues acts, such as The Blackberry Booze Band, The Sundance Blues Band, Fate and Blue Midnight. Solo acoustic artists and country bands also filled the venue's tiny stage. The Bruce Springsteen Band played the club on numerous occasions.

Though it was more than modest in length, the venue was only about 45 feet wide.

"You would go in the door and there was a 25 seat bar on the left and to the right was the stage," Amato said.

The stage, higher in comparison to other clubs of its size, stood behind a small dance floor and some tables placed throughout the venue. The club's sparse décor mainly consisted of mirrors.

"It was just your average gin mill," Schraeger said.

IN CAHOOTS, IN ASBURY PARK

Music fans packed the small venue on Friday and Saturday nights. Slightly diminished crowds still visited The Student Prince on other nights.

During a snowy night in 1973, Matthews walked from Bradley Beach, a shore town a few miles south of Asbury, to see Springsteen at the Student Prince just after the release of "Greetings from Asbury Park, N.J." The band played in front of a small crowd, after playing cities in places such as Virginia and Pennsylvania, Matthews said. It wasn't Matthews' only trip to the venue.

"We used to go there and dance to the Bank Street Blues band all of the time," he said.

Similar in layout but twice the size was **The Alamo**, which was located on the corner of Third and Kingsley avenues. The "basic corner bar" mainly hosted southern and standard rock bands, Amato said. The Alamo's stage was lower than that of The Student Prince. In the middle of the venue was a bar that was surrounded by seats. The square-shaped establishment was twice the size of The Student Prince and could fit between 200-250 inside. It did most of its business from Wednesday through Saturday nights, but wasn't among Asbury Park's most popular bars. Though Schraeger played at the club once with Dayz, he and his Cahoots bandmates didn't spend much time at the bar. Bobby Bertelson's band, White Kracker, frequently performed songs by Bad Company, Yes and other rock music at The Alamo. The band's guitarist would lay his axe on an ironing board as if he were playing a pedal steel without sonically emulating the instrument, said Tim O'Neill, who currently runs one of the Jersey Shore's hottest clubs, Bar Anticipation, in Lake Como. Bobby Bertelson danced across The Alamo's stage, earning adoration from the opposite sex, he said.

"He was like a showman, more than a singer," O'Neill said.

The Alamo only survived for about two years. It reopened as **One**

Josh Davidson

Sane Man and closed again after one year. Many other Asbury Park clubs met the same fate, staying open for a couple of years before reopening with a new owner. The occurrence became more frequent after The Stone Pony opened in 1974.

"How could you compete with The Pony?" Amato said. "You had The Pony, which knocked out a lot of stuff in Asbury."

The Roman Arch, on Ocean Avenue, hosted bands that played lounge music.

"Bands that would roll into The Gold Digger and The Roman Arch would play for an entire week," said O'Neill, describing some of Asbury Park's lounge clubs. "They wouldn't come in for a one-night stand."

The club was preceded by **Steve Brody's** and later became **Julio's South,** after the owners of a northern Jersey venue called Julio's purchased the club. The Julio's owners changed the music format into mainstream top 40, pop and disco music.

"They tried to make Julio's South a mainstream club that played what was popular, but it was really harder to compete with The Pony, because The Pony had a built-in crowd at the time," O'Neill said. "They had a great lineup and something going on every day of the week."

Other than the lounge music venues, such as The Gold Digger, which opened early in the afternoon, the majority of Asbury Park's clubs did not open until 9 p.m., O'Neill said. The bands and their staff members used the afternoon to set up and prepare for the evening, without an audience.

"The clubs would not open the doors until everything was done and perfect, because they didn't want to charge a cover only to have customers come in and watch people working to set up for the night," he said. "That's not how they did things back then."

The Wonder Bar also opened for most of the day, selling hot dogs and burgers out of its front window.

IN CAHOOTS, IN ASBURY PARK

On any given weekend in the 1970s, **Convention Hall** was place where fans could see two or possibly three rock n' roll legends like Janus Joplin, The Who and The Doors in an intimate, 3,600-seat setting. By the mid-1980s, they could only see a handful of mediocre heavy metal bands at the venue. The lure of the venue already gave way to The Garden State Arts Center, in Holmdel, in the mid-1970s. But Convention Hall got a reprieve when the Arts Center banned rock n' roll shows due to a riot during one of its concerts. For a brief time span, major acts returned to Convention Hall, while soft rock bands, such as Air Supply, played at the Arts Center. Still, The Arts Center and arenas like the Brendan Byrne Arena, in East Rutherford, New Jersey, provided about 15,000 more seats to fill, significantly increasing the profits for major acts.

The exterior of The Sunshine Inn in 1979. (Photo by Lewis Bloom)
While The Stone Pony dominated the scene, venues like **The Wonder Bar** and **Sunshine Inn** brought in more than respectable crowds. Located across from Convention Hall at 1213 Ocean Avenue (on the

corner of 5th and Ocean Avenues), **The Wonder Bar** could fit about 300 Top 40s rock n' roll fans between its walls in the 1970s. After entering the venue and turning left, fans would notice a huge bar that spanned along its entire back wall. One of the highest stages in the city was surrounded by a railing and located behind the bar.

"So lifting a B-3 or any kind of organ to get it on that stage was no easy feat," said Amato, who played at the club prior to his days with Brothers and Sisters.

Matthews interacted more closely with many of today's classic rock artists when he lived at **The Sunshine Inn** in 1971. Located just footsteps west of the Stone Pony, The Sunshine Inn was a former bus garage converted into a large warehouse, which consisted of nothing more than a stage. Eventually, a small section of bleachers were added on the opposite end of the stage, but it was standing room only for most visitors.

The activity inside was mostly dormant until its owner could rustle up enough money to bring in a major label act like Black Sabbath, Peter Frampton, Rainbow, Cactus or Kiss. The Sunshine Inn hosted mostly hosted national acts, but invited some local bands to perform on occasion. Though the club was built to fit about 1,800 people, the promoters usually managed to squeeze in about 3,000 young and inebriated concert goers.

Most bands brought in their own sound systems since the club didn't own one. Others asked Tinker West, Steel Mill's manager, to bring his system and run sound. West was intelligent and had a strong knowledge of business, Matthews said. He was nearly 40 and served as a father figure to the musicians and fans, he said.

"He had been around the block a few times," Matthews said.

Kiss performed at The Warehouse from 1973-1974, as they began to gain notoriety nationally. Employed as an electrician at the club in 1973,

IN CAHOOTS, IN ASBURY PARK

Matthews became concerned when the band's members explained its plan to bring in pyrotechnics. He stared at the old, dry wood ceiling and thought the club would certainly go up in flames. The combination of fireworks and the large parachute that hung over the stage as a canopy didn't sit well with him.

"I thought for sure that they were going to set the building on fire, but they didn't," he said.

Matthews was hired to keep the venue from catching fire, which it had done on repeated prior occasions. The venue's owner paid him $35 and all of the beer he could consume to stand near a circuit panel in the back of the Inn and ensure the power would not overload. He configured all of the Inn's electrical components.

Matthews met Black Sabbath's singer, Ozzy Osbourne, at the club. Though Osbourne and his band mates had a reputation for mayhem, they did not cause trouble at the venue. Schraeger saw the fusion legends Mahavishnu Orchestra and blues-rocker Edgar Winter at the venue. Asbury Park's **boardwalk casino** also hosted national acts like ZZ Top, who Schraeger saw in 1973. The boardwalk casino closed in 1988. The amusements portion of the facility was demolished in May 2004.

"Asbury always had a good flux of music going on," Amato said. "That's what the town was about, no matter where you went."

Located on the corner of 2nd and Kingsley Avenues, **Club Zulu**, also known as the African Room, was one of the city's few venues that featured jazz music. Amato snuck into the club with friends of his father when he was 12.

"That is where I first met Brothers and Sisters," Amato said. "They were all older than me. Eventually I saw them again at the Roman Arch and ended up in the band." Even prior to the 1970s, music fans packed establishments like the **Lincoln Hotel** where they shuffled their feet to Buzzy Soul playing drums to jazz records. As time progressed, folk artist

Josh Davidson

Melanie was accompanied by Ricky DeSarno downstairs at the original **Inkwell**. Throughout its history, Asbury's stages have produced pages of history and legendary tales that will be told for generations to come.

Works Cited

Staff report. *Asbury Park Riots Report.* Red Bank, NJ. *The Daily Register,* 1970. Print. This work was cited for background regarding the Asbury Park riots in the **Preface** of *In Cahoots, In Asbury Park.*

Chantal Pike, Helen. *Asbury Park: Where Music Lives.* Asbury Park, NJ. Asbury Park Zone Development Corporation/Clayton Press, 2011. This work was cited for background regarding Sonny Kenn in **Chapter 2** of *In Cahoots, In Asbury Park.*

Santelli, Robert. *Greetings from E Street: The Story of Bruce Springsteen and the E Street Band.* San Francisco, CA. Chronicle Books, 2006. Print. This work was cited for background regarding Bruce Springsteen's early career in **Chapters 2 and 11** of *In Cahoots, In Asbury Park*, though my interviews with Mr. Santelli were used throughout this book.

CBS Coverage. *Southside Johnny & The Asbury Jukes' Debut Album Release Party: Stone Pony, Asbury Park - 1976.* Asbury Park, New Jersey. CBS,1976. Video. This work was cited for background regarding Southside Johnny & The Asbury Jukes' famous 1976 Stone Pony show in **Chapter 14** of *In Cahoots, In Asbury Park.*

Josh Davidson

Orlean, Susan. *Bon Jovi: The Kids are Alright.* New York, NY. *Rolling Stone Magazine*, 1987. Print. This work was cited for background regarding Bon Jovi's early career in **Chapter 26** of *In Cahoots, In Asbury Park*.

Photo Credits

Front Cover. Taken by Slevin, Michelle. *Asbury Park Boardwalk Casino.*

Back Cover. Taken by Bloom, Lewis. *Exterior of the Sunshine Inn, Asbury Park, New Jersey, in 1979.*

Chapter One. Courtesy of Ferrera, Lisa. *Cahoots in the late 1970s.* Page 10.

Chapter Two. Taken by Bloom, Lewis. *Upper Deck of the Fun House, Asbury Park.* Page 22.

Chapter Five. Courtesy of Mueller, Ed. *Green Mermaid and Upstage.* Pages 57-58, 60 and 64.

Chapter Seven. Taken by Bloom, Lewis. *John Luraschi photo.* Page 80.

Chapter Eight. Taken by Bloom, Lewis. *Tony Amato photo.* Page 89.

Chapter Nine. Courtesy of Schraeger, Steve. *Photo of Steve Schraeger and Gene Krupa.* Page 93. Taken by Bloom, Lewis. *Steve Schraeger photo.* Page 95.

Chapter Ten. Taken by Bloom, Lewis. *John Oeser photo.* Page 103.

Chapter Twelve. Taken by Bloom, Lewis. *Tony Amato photo.* Page 118. Courtesy of Amato, Tony. *Cahoots in the late 1970s.* Page 120.

Chapter Fourteen. Taken by Bloom, Lewis. *Bruce Springsteen and "Southside" Johnny Lyon photo.* Page 132. *Photos of the Shakes.* Pages 135 and 137. *Photo of Vini Lopez.* Page 139.

Josh Davidson

Chapter Fifteen. Courtesy of Schraeger, Steve. *Photo of Schraeger and George Theiss outside of The Stone Pony in Asbury Park.* Page 144.

Taken by Bloom, Lewis. *John Oeser photo.* Page 145.

Chapter Seventeen. Courtesy of Hannan, Joy. *Photo of Hannan and Tony Amato in the late 1970s.* Page 164. Taken by Freestone, Conni. *Photo of Hannan and Amato in 2013.* Page 166.

Chapter Eighteen. Taken by Bloom, Lewis. *Photo of the Shakes.* Page 174.

Chapter Twenty-One. Promotional photo. *Photo of The George Theiss Band.* Page 200.

Chapter Twenty-Two. Taken by Bloom, Lewis. *Photo of the Shots.* Page 205.

Chapter Twenty-Three. Taken by Freestone, Conni. *Photos of Tony Amato and Steve Schraeger at The Stone Pony.* Page 225. Courtesy of Amato, Marsha. *Photo of John Oeser's 60th Birthday.* Page 228.

Chapter Twenty-Five. Taken by Bloom, Lewis. *Photo of the Asbury Park boardwalk in 1981.* Page 241. Taken by Freestone, Conni. *Photo of former members of Cahoots* (Page 249) and p*hoto of John Oeser's dress hat (*Page 250).

Chapter Twenty-Six. Taken by Bloom, Lewis. *Photo of the exterior of the Sunshine Inn in 1979.* Page 260.

Acknowledgements

The author extends a special thanks to the following individuals who contributed their time, photos, knowledge, talent, stories and insight into one of the most important cities in rock n' roll history:

Cahoots' Members

Tony Amato, Tommy LaBella, John Luraschi, Steve Schraeger, Michael Scialfa and George Theiss

Club Owners and Staff

Lisa Ferrara, Lee Mrowicki, Tim "Squeaky" O'Neill and Scott Stamper

Design Consulting

Michael Burke

Editor

Karl Vilacoba

Experts and Historians

Eileen Chapman, Tom Gilmour, Charles Horner, Robert Santelli and Henry Vaccaro, Sr.

Supporters of the City and Music Scene

Marsha Amato, Joan Cambria, Joy Hannan, Rich Kelly, Tom Matthews, Ray Maxwell, Ed Mueller and Carol Wuestoff

Josh Davidson

New Jersey Musicians

Ernest "Boom" Carter, Billy Hector, Suzan Lastovica, Jeremy Mykietyn, Paul Nelson and Al "Albee" Tellone

Photographers

Lewis Bloom, Conni Freestone and Michelle Slevin

About the Author

Josh Davidson is a former staff writer and New Jersey Press Association Better Newspaper Contest first place award winner for Gannett Co., Inc. and Greater Media Newspapers' publications. He has written thousands of articles on topics ranging from music, military, municipal governments, investigative reporting/crime, sports and news for hundreds of publications. *The New York Times* once called an article he wrote for *Jersey Beat Magazine*, "A well-researched article...which pulls readers towards the pulse of the Asbury rock music scene."

He is the co-founder and former managing editor of the New Jersey-based online rock magazine, *Chorus and Verse*. He is also an accomplished lead singer/guitarist and songwriter who has performed in venues throughout the tri-state area, including The Stone Pony and Bitter End.

Davidson grew up in Freehold, New Jersey, and now resides in Baltimore, Maryland. A former civilian public affairs director for a multi-billion dollar United States Army organization, Davidson is currently director of proposals & solutioning for Adams Communication & Engineering Technology, Inc., at Aberdeen Proving Ground, Maryland. He has received the Department of the Army's Achievement Medal for Civilian Service and Commander's Award for Civilian Service.

Josh Davidson

Made in the USA
Middletown, DE
18 April 2019